Modern Local Government

WITHDRAWN FROM STOCK

Modern Local Government

Janice Morphet

SAGE Publications
Los Angeles • London • New Delhi • Singapore

© Janice Morphet 2008

First published 2008

Apart from any fair dealing for the purposes of research or private study, or criticism or review, as permitted under the Copyright, Designs and Patents Act, 1988, this publication may be reproduced, stored or transmitted in any form, or by any means, only with the prior permission in writing of the publishers, or in the case of reprographic reproduction, in accordance with the terms of licences issued by the Copyright Licensing Agency. Enquiries concerning reproduction outside those terms should be sent to the publishers.

SAGE Publications Ltd
1 Oliver's Yard
55 City Road
London EC1Y 1SP

SAGE Publications Inc.
2455 Teller Road
Thousand Oaks, California 91320

SAGE Publications India Pvt Ltd
B 1/I 1 Mohan Cooperative Industrial Area
Mathura Road
New Delhi 110 044

SAGE Publications Asia-Pacific Pte Ltd
33 Pekin Street #02-01
Far East Square
Singapore 048763

Library of Congress Control Number: 2007940155

British Library Cataloguing in Publication data

A catalogue record for this book is available from the British Library

ISBN 978–0–7619–4374–7
ISBN 978–0–7619–4375–4 (pbk)

Typeset by Newgen Imaging Systems (P) Ltd, Chennai, India
Printed in Great Britain by Athenaeum Press, Gateshead, Tyne & Wear
Printed on paper from sustainable resources

To Robin, Sophie and Charlotte

Contents

Preface

The pace and scale of reform in local government always seems unremitting to those close to it. For a long period before 1997, the reforms all appeared to be focused on reducing the power and central role of local authorities, both in their democratic leadership of their communities and in being the first point of contact between citizens and government. The changes since 1997 have seen more reforms but, 10 years on, these are seen to be leading somewhere, stages on a journey that could take local government back to a point of local leadership, co-ordination, and direction. In their individual ways these reforms are frequently difficult to understand, and each has a life cycle that initially seems to introduce a very demanding target, which, after incorporation, provides the platform for the next stage of change. As a result of their response to this unremitting change, local authorities are now seen to be leaders of cultural transformation and improvement in the public sector. Local authorities still have much to do but are more confident about how to set about change and how to assess its impact on people's lives.

The scale of this change, the length of the route map – currently stretching to 2014 – is frequently overlooked in its entirety; there is an overarching direction although it seems very difficult for most to see it. There are problems on the way as well as excursions, diversions, blind alleys, and 'highwaymen' which all serve to feed weekly media but distract from a focus on the future. Sometimes these diversions almost seem intended to disguise other intents. This book is an attempt to set out some of the key elements of the reform agenda including the drivers for change before 1997 which still propel future actions. Understanding the way in which the reforms have been generated may provide some tools to understand the plan as a whole.

This book is also written to allow both central and local government perspectives on local government reform to be understood. There is little that is written about local government from a central government perspective apart from the formal policy documents which appear regularly. Through these an attempt is made to understand what the centre is thinking and the direction the centre sees for the local. Local government attempts to translate this policy into action. Those who write about local government seldom see an overall picture. Some become specialists in particular fields while, for those working in local government, every proposed change, coming as it does in an initially over-prescribed format, seems too much, and an attempt to undermine local government. What is clear is that the overall role and standing of local government has changed in this period, and for local government, an inability to recognise this could result in a failure to take opportunities and to provide much needed advice on successful policy implementation to central government. This approach has also meant that it is difficult for those coming new to local government to understand what is occurring – students, academics, and practitioners have little to use which can provide an overarching narrative. This book also fills this gap.

The germ of this book started when I was asked to give a presentation to a group of civil servants new to working with local government. The task was to provide them with an understanding of the system, the pressures, and the recent extent of change. This regular slot continued for a few years and started to be used with other groups and some postgraduate students. As time went by, it was clear that the gap between the reality of change at the local level and the understanding of this by academics and others was growing, and I was invited to write this book. During the time of writing much more has changed and helpful comments on the text have shown that the scale and speed of this catches many readers unawares. I hope that the book does fill some of these gaps and that, despite the jargon-filled world that we all live in, it is possible to make sense of what is here. I have tried to make each chapter reasonably self-contained, knowing that readers plunder texts for their immediate needs and I hope that this does not lead to unnecessary repetition for those who are more interested in an end-to-end read.

As ever, many thanks are due. First to Phil Allmendinger who invited me to write this book and has given continuing support as has Mark Tewdwr-Jones. I have found their assumptions useful in helping me set out my own views. Thanks also go to Chris Bellamy who has provided many useful and detailed comments on the text, taking time from her own major project to do so and for this I am very grateful. Other thanks go to Jane Foulsham and Andrew Whetnall who both had a role in helping me to develop a civil service perspective on these changes after I had spent nearly thirty years in local government. Of course, all opinions, errors, and omissions are mine. Finally thanks to Robin, Sophie, and Charlotte who put up with my constant tapping but who also bring their own considerable insights to the central–local relationship which are always revealing.

Janice Morphet
Wandsworth 2007

1

INTRODUCTION

Why another book on local government? The answer to this question is simple. Since 1997, local government has changed more than at any time since the 1880s. Although those who have lived through the reorganisation of local authority boundaries in 1963, 1972, 1987, and the 1990s might argue that these changes were more significant; since the 1997 general election local decision making, the power of elected councillors and role of local government have all changed. In the past, local authorities were 'creatures' of statute, unable to undertake any activity unless specifically enabled. Now, although they do not have a general power of competence, the duty of a local authority to promote the well-being of its area, together with accompanying powers, mark a key change. Local trading has now re-emerged, and the review of local government finance will encourage new ways of raising local taxation.

Yet, much of the press coverage and academic reflection of local government suggest that it remains under siege. Proposals for the reform of Children's Services are seen to be part of a major strategy for power and control of local government by the central government Department responsible. Concerns are said to be expressed by the Department for Transport that it was losing the local war for funding to children and social care and that this encouraged re-examination of central control for the ring fencing of transport funding. The continuation of central targetry does nothing for joined-up working at the local level or provide the basis for action to meet local needs.

In all of this, local government continues to consider itself to be the victim. If it steps out of line, even with new freedoms and flexibilities, it assumes that there are sanctions from central government departments. The Local Government Association calls this a 'grudgingly instrumentalist' approach (LGA 2003b). Although the 'centre' is seen to support local democracy for directly elected health or police committees (Blears 2003), local authority democracy does not seem to be as attractive as dedicated single-purpose boards in helping central government departments to achieve their local targets. David Miliband challenged local authorities to come forward with their own brand of neighbourhood solutions in his double devolution formula (Miliband 2006a, 2006b).

How has local government coped with these changes since 1997? Has it been able to join up at the local level despite more 'silo-based targetry' from its central government partners (Perri 6 et al. 2002)? How can local government regenerate a sense of its own worth – a reconnection with civic pride and renewal which is most frequently associated with Joseph Chamberlain's Birmingham of the 1880s (Marsh 1994)? Local government does not have to fight for recognition elsewhere in the world where its role in government is enshrined in written constitutions and where local authorities do not have to seek specific legal permission to act. Does this make local government more effective and the centre weaker? If proposals to move central departments out of London were progressed as a result of the Lyons's *Independent Review* (Lyons 2004), would this coincide with downsizing their functions?

This book considers the structure and functions of local government after a major period of reform and offers a reassessment of its role. It provides a means of understanding how these reforms work with the existing services and in an increasingly connected way. Rather than seeing these reforms as instrumentalist, the book argues that local government is moving to an international norm for local governance within the state. Given the continuing pace of change, it offers an analytical framework within which future changes can be understood.

As with any change, there is always a distinction to be made between underlying trends and influences and those that attract daily media interest. At times, when a particularly strong news story breaks, it is hard to make any sense of the general direction of change. Local government is as prone to short-run stories as any other form of politics. These long- and short-term trends sometimes coincide and at other times collide. However, it is important to understand the role of both in change.

Why local government?

To find the answer to this question, many commentators have turned to the last reform of local government in the late 1880s. Why was it seen to be necessary then and have we lost our way now? For many, the legacy of Joseph Chamberlain in Birmingham, or other civic pioneers, seems to hold the key. In the 1920s and 1930s, Winifred Holtby's novel *South Riding* holds no rosy view of local government but still defines it as being the first line of defence against poverty (Holtby 1936). At the same time, Anderson was writing about corruption and dishonesty in local government in *Rotten Borough* (1937), a fictional account based on Grantham, the home of Mrs Thatcher and her father, who was an alderman of the council around the time this novel was written.

Birmingham provides one of the best examples of civic purpose and renewal for which people are now searching. Through the leadership of

Joseph Chamberlain, Birmingham was given a strong sense of civic direction. Chamberlain was elected as mayor between 1873 and 1876. His impact during this time was significant and was to have a long-lasting influence on local government:

> During this time Chamberlain successfully widened the scope of local government from which there would be no withdrawal for over a century. The Town Council would be an instrument of collective purpose. Quite simply he set himself the task of governing Birmingham in the interests of the whole community; he was a radical elected on a populist ticket. (Cherry 1994, p. 77)

Chamberlain's leadership resulted in many major areas of the city being re-developed, including Corporation Street, the Town Hall, and libraries. Some of these changes were in order to promote the increased health of the city but Chamberlain was also interested in the city's economy and the happiness of its people.

How far were the changes which occurred in Birmingham and other major cities representative of a contemporary picture? Did they reflect a debate about central and local power? Did they provide a means of supporting a more urbanised society that was a necessary part of economic growth and may now be difficult to fully comprehend? What is clear is that for the period between 1880 and 1900, local government in England was confident. It made huge strides in improvement works and built a large number of new town halls (Cunningham 1981), schools, and libraries. Local authorities took over inner city country houses and turned them into public parks. They built drains, lit streets, and ran public transport on a scale unseen before. Yet, they did not do everything. They did not build as many houses as were expected (Young and Garside 1983). Poor relief was still seen to be a service run on early nineteenth-century principles of shame which were not to be removed until the post-1945 era. Councillors, mayors, and town clerks (Headrick 1962) were seen to be important civic leaders. Local government was benevolent and paternal.

Local authorities are the place of first resort in any community when individuals need information or are confronted with problems such as flooding. There is a general assumption that their role is to support local communities. The period between 1945 and 1974 saw this community support role being primarily delivered through homes, schools, roads, and in the provision of other social infrastructure. The period after 1974 required a different approach. The economic crisis meant that there was little funding to continue investment. The same trends were working on local economies as industrial restructuring began in earnest in a phase that did not finish until the early 1990s. Local authorities were on the front line, but they required very different skills. The large departments of architects and engineers were no longer needed and new roles in regeneration and community capacity building were required. This transition period extended over time with some local authorities taking longer to adjust than others. There was an initial period of shock that formerly wealthy industrial cities such as Birmingham and

Manchester could suffer the same kind of decline as others with more traditional industries.

This change also meant an adjustment in style for central government. The large building programme in the post-war era had provided a direct link between local and central government through capital expenditure and funding programmes. The relationships were clear and rewards for delivery were high with more funding at the local level. Post-1974, the skills required at the local level were softer and required a much greater degree of coordination. The larger metropolitan authorities took a strategic approach to these issues, and the newly created district councils developed a new agenda which had a more practical, localised approach. Many larger councils adopted 'neighbourhoodisation' in the early 1980s to respond to the needs of their communities through management and delivery of services at the local level. For central government, the response eventually turned to another major initiative – the implementation of competition and encouragement of local authorities to be more efficient in their operations.

Central government was also going through changes with the creation of Next Steps Agencies and Non-departmental Public Bodies in an effort to respond to the impact of competition on its responsibilities. Major utilities were sold off. These pressures for change, deriving in part from the 1994 General Agreement on Tariffs and Trade (GATT) to open up public services to the private sector were similar to those for competition in local government.

When central government wanted to respond with action at the local level, both Mrs Thatcher's anti-local government views and the centre's dislike of 'fragmented' local government led to the generation of specific organisations to undertake local programmes – task forces, Urban Development Corporations, and quangos (Lawless 1989). By the mid-1990s, local authorities lacked confidence and many years of low investment. Concentration on urban regeneration activities had distracted some from the emergence of specific social and community issues. Standards of attainment in schools were not keeping pace with other parts of the world. Hospital care was also seen to be in a lower division than other European countries and investment in public transport had reduced to a minimal level. At local level funding for roads, maintenance was often redirected to deal with leaking school roofs. England had also become multicultural in this 20-year period in a way which was almost unnoticed. These issues created a major agenda to be dealt with in 1997, although at the time it was uncertain whether either local or central government appreciated the scale of this task.

The debate on central–local relations

The importance of the role of 'local' government has been examined frequently. Many theorists take a critical view of centralism and focus on local government as a counterweight or alternative to the growing power of central government. As Pickvance and Preteceille (1991b) state, local government can only be seen or understood within the state as a whole. Restructuring local government cannot be undertaken without changing the nature of the total state. Devolution has the same effect. Much of the literature about local government that is used as the touchstone for understanding and analysis was generated during the anti-local government period 1979–1997. Even after 1997, the critical emphasis is on the domination of local government by external management styles, and competition is viewed as an assault on the public sector ethic. Post 1997 refocusing has attracted little attention. Local government is not dominated by a sense of privatisation. Rather, since 1997, local government has been dominated by an overwhelming focus on targets and performance which have been increasingly and more successfully focused towards citizen outcomes including improved health, increased educational qualifications, and better housing management. Indeed, to read that a focus on outcome is not as beneficial as a concentration on process (Kakabadse et al. 2003) can now read like a plea for professional or producer dominance over people-based outcomes.

The context of local government reform

The programme for the 'modernisation' of local government in England began in 1997 when the Labour government took power. The incoming government had a full change agenda for local government, which was based both on concerns and its potential as the direct deliverer of 80% of all public services. Under previous Conservative administrations, local government had been increasingly directed from central government with ever-larger proportions of their budgets 'passported' by central departments, directed towards the achievement of specific targets notably in social services and education. This inevitably produced a tight financial squeeze on other public services, such as roads, parks, planning, and environmental protection, which were frequently now bracketed together as the 'liveability' agenda. The public also increasingly expressed concerns that local authorities were not responsive to local people and that they had a culture that was not adequately focused on performance related to their needs.

The 1997 Labour government was concerned about democratic engagement with lower turnout rates in elections and particularly low involvement in the democratic process by young people. Additionally there were growing fears about the potential for council corruption which was confirmed through the 'Donnygate' case, where in Doncaster leading elected council members were convicted for accepting bribes and favours in return for planning consents. Finally from the councils' perspective, increasing efforts to privatise or outsource council services were seen as an anathema to the public service tradition.

In 1997, this wide reform agenda for English local government was pulled together as a programme to modernise local government and, as the local government minister commented in 2004, this has been a 10-year project of radical change, not incremental tinkering (Mulholland 2004). The incoming government quickly published a series of white papers and other consultation reports, which were soon followed by the Local Government Act 1999 and the Local Government Act 2000. These acts, which covered different elements of the modernisation agenda, were directed to

1 ensure that councils' political decision-making processes are efficient, transparent, and accountable;
2 continuously improve the efficiency and quality of the services for which they are responsible;
3 actively involve and engage the community in local decisions;
4 have the powers they need to work with other bodies to ensure that resources are deployed effectively to improve the well-being of their areas.

The main themes of the post-1997 period, then, were set and emerged in a variety of ways through legislation, specific initiatives, and funding. Issues such as performance and competition were included in best value, and after 2004, through the efficiency agenda. Other elements of the modernisation agenda were included in the Local Government Act 2000 which primarily dealt with the implementation of new council constitutions; the duty to promote economic, social, and environmental well-being; and the preparation of a Community Strategy. Other major components included proposals to establish Local Strategic Partnerships (LSP) (DTLR 2001c), e-government (ODPM 2003g), and Local Public Service Agreements (LPSAs) (ODPM/LGA 2003), all of which have been implemented without legislative underpinning.

These modernising reforms have worked their way through local government. Further white papers on local government were published: 'Strong Local leadership – Quality Public Services' in December 2001 and 'Strong and Prosperous Communities' in October 2006. The first concentrated primarily on the delivery agenda – performance, leadership, finance, e-government, LPSAs, and working together with central government around the citizen. It also made some commitments to reduce the total plan requirements which central government makes of local government. It stated that local authorities produced some 66 plans at the government's behest. Some authorities had longer lists than this – perhaps double the number when strategies, statements, and other regular submissions of this kind were included. Almost none of these is joined up across issue, geography, or departments. There was a commitment to halve them. Further, those councils which were seen to perform well were promised further freedoms.

The latest round of local government reform builds on this earlier establishment of joined-up working with public agencies and proposes that there should a duty of public bodies to cooperate. Local authorities are seen to have a new role of place-shaping proposed by Lyons in 2006 and endorsed in the subsequent Local Government White Paper (2006) that involves bringing together all the public services in their areas. It also identifies the role of city regions in the future economic growth of the country and how these might be set up using Multi-Area Agreements (MAAs). It also contains a more localised approach to a performance framework that joins up more with other public agencies at the local level. Finally it proposes parishing for the whole country including urban areas and the potential devolution of services to this level.

How do they do it elsewhere?

Elsewhere in the world, local government has more legal autonomy (Hewison 2001) and certainly feels less pressurised by central government. Many local authorities have more freedom to act and more ability to raise funding, from taxation or other means. Local government in Great Britain is still seen as part of the national machinery of government. Its elections are seen to be a judgement on the state of national politics. Yet, the local level is one of the main interests in post-1991 Europe. Osterland (1994) argues that as the local level is the one which most affects people, and is the most important in post-reunification Germany, 'the restructuring of local government in its various dimensions is an aspect of state restructuring in general' (Pickvance and Preteille 1991b, p. 3).

In Australia and New Zealand, the local governance system and powers were inherited from Great Britain, but more recently there has been a range of legislation to change these systems and now the reform of local government in England has been based on the New Zealand reforms introduced in 1989. As in the United Kingdom, local authorities had been enabled to act through specific legislative powers rather than to operate within a national constitutional framework. A discussion on the potential benefits which could be engendered through the provision of a general power of competence began in New Zealand in 1985, when the issue of local authorities being able to act in the interests of their citizens was raised (Hewison 2001). Since the reforms of local government in New Zealand, more concentration has been placed on the role of local government community leadership rather than on the role of local authorities as service providers.

In 1997, there were a number of different influences on the prime minister's approach to government and governance. These influences would have obvious implications for reforming local government not least given the fears of its potential to become the incoming government's Achilles' heel. The two main external sources were 'The Third Way' (Giddens 1998) and 'Reinventing Government', an approach developed by Vice President Al Gore in 1992 (Osborne and Gaebler 1992). These were important influences and remain so today albeit in new forms. 'Reinventing Government' has been superseded by 'The Price of Government' (Osborne and Hutchinson 2004) whereas Giddens's approach has been supplemented by Robert Putnam's notions of social capital (2000).

The notion of social capital

The continuing and rising concerns of politicians about voter apathy and low turnout rates have led to a greater consideration of the ways in which communities can be more actively engaged in participation in local affairs. Much of the post-1997 agenda for local government has been designed to encourage greater participation whether on new council constitutions, mayoral referenda, user feedback in best value, and more active neighbourhood engagement through decentralised working. In addition to the important link between voter turnout and political legitimation, there have also been concerns about the more general decline in community engagement that this might signal. Robert Putnam's notion that 'better together' (Putnam et al. 2003) is better than 'bowling alone' (2000) is based on research on the decline in participation of all kinds of voluntary and community bodies in the United States in the period since 1945. Putnam argues that social capital is being undermined by this gradual decline and that if allowed to continue then civic life and any attempt to encourage more participation within it will fall even further. This is seen by Putnam to be an important underpinning for social cohesion and community self-management.

As Putnam (2000, p. 19) states, the core notion of social capital is that social networks have value, which influence the productivity of individuals and groups. Without these networks, Putnam argues that individuals become more isolated and lose the experience and expectation that working for their communities represents a valued role. This also includes the development of mutual relationships, where rules of conduct can be developed which help in creating norms of reciprocity. Putnam also argues that these networks and participation in reciprocal relationships lead to the development of trust – a commodity which politicians in the United Kingdom perceive to be in short supply. Putnam demonstrates his thesis of social capital through a variety of case studies and also shows that this social capital can be used for malevolent purposes, particularly in societies where networks exert other forms of social control or behaviours which are harmful.

Although Putnam's thesis is generally accepted, that is, that community empowerment and engagement are generally encouraged by participation in networks, there is also evidence in the United Kingdom that participation rates are very high in all kinds of voluntary, community, and interest organisations. Carvel (2006) reports that an average Briton belongs to 17 organisations. These activities range from sports and social clubs, volunteering, and helping at a child's school. However, although these activities are seen to be contributing to social capital, they are not recognised by those who are engaged in them as participative in the political sense of the word. People in the United Kingdom also have more active networks of friends than other countries and are also more likely to participate in community activity. Putnam's notion has become influential and understood in the United Kingdom as a generalised principle although the evidence of participation does not seem to be similar to the U.S. trends.

The relationship between local performance and the economy

In the second term of the Labour government, 2001–2005, Putnam's notions of 'social capital' were more dominant, using social cohesion as one of the main means of improving the performance of the British economy. The influence of performance-based approaches, derived from Washington, have also been significant, with the view that central government has become too large and is now hampering the economic health of the state.

This approach has since developed further into a greater interest in the relationship between the scale of government and its performance. On the one hand, better performance management could be a necessary prerequisite to 'letting go' and downsizing. On the other hand, performance management may displace other more traditional central government tasks, such as policy making, but not lead to smaller government, just the same number of people undertaking different tasks. This debate on the relationship between performance and scale has been taken forward in *The Price of Government* (2004), where Osborne and Hutchinson argue that government activity should be more focused on key priorities and results rather than on maintaining *status quo*. In this way, energies can be focused on what is important and costs can be reduced. Their views are fuelled by the scale of the fiscal crisis in local and central government in the United States. This approach is generating a radical review of the size of government everywhere and it is useful to consider these principles to be contributing drivers to what is being translated as the movement to 'new localism' (see Chapter 10) and 'devolved decision making' in England (HMT 2004a, 2004b, 2006). Osborne and Hutchinson set out these principles as 10 operational activities to create efficient government, which are

1 Strategic reviews – divesting to invest by combing through programmes and identifying redundancy.
2 Consolidation – rather than concentrating on merging organisations, which take time and reduce delivery effectiveness through the confusion they cause, rather merge budgets and put them in the hands of 'steering' organisations which purchase from 'rowing' or provider organisations which may be from any sector.
3 Rightsizing – understanding that the right size is critical for the success of some activities, but this does not mean 'one size fits all'.
4 Buying services competitively – making public institutions compete with other sectors can save money.
5 Rewarding performance not good intentions – in this way those who improve their outcomes receive higher rewards.
6 Smarter customer service – putting customers in the driving seat introducing more choice and more appropriate means of delivery to suit the service and the customer.
7 Don't buy mistrust – eliminate it – win voluntary compliance rather than generate rules which people will attempt to evade or cheat.

8 Using flexibility to get accountability – encourage more freedoms and flexibilities for those who accept more performance-based structures.

9 Making administrative systems allies not enemies – organisations are prisoners of their internal systems and these have to be modernised and streamlined which can generate major savings.

10 Smarter work processes: tools from industry – organisations need to change the way in which they work using a variety of tools including Total Quality Management (TQM), Business Process Reengineering (BPR), and team Workouts or small problem-solving groups brought together for fixed periods. (Osborne and Hutchinson 2004, pp. 13–17)

All of these approaches have had an important underlying influence on the relative relationship between central and local states. The dominant thesis emerging is that the centre is too large and that without devolving responsibility to the local level, democratic engagement will be further reduced while the national economy will fail to grow at the levels required to be competitive (HMT 2004b). These are very significant changes and are unprecedented in the history of central–local relationships. They have influenced policy making for local government since 1997 and continue to do so.

Conclusions

The range and pace of change in local governance has been extensive since 1997 with further changes in the pipeline on funding, sub-local authority governance structures, joint procurement, and joint public service delivery boards being proposed across local geographies. The reform of local government since 1997 in the United Kingdom is significant and is understood as such by those in other countries, although in the United Kingdom it is often regarded as a series of piecemeal initiatives. These reforms combine into a significant and strategic framework for the future.

2

GREAT EXPECTATIONS – THE POSITION IN 1997

intro /spending

Introduction

The election success of a Labour government in 1997, its scale and manner, brought with it both a significant degree of expectation and 'baggage'. From the perspective of local authorities, the long period during which they had many of their powers removed and their role reduced was over. Local authorities considered that their right to govern had been undermined (Stoker 2004) and had been taken over by both central government and a series of quangos. Additionally, there was a view that local government's role was increasingly being invaded by the private sector and that increasing pressure on delivery was being accompanied by reduced funding. Local authorities remained dependent on central government for their annual financial allocations and the tax which they were allowed to levy. In the post-1997 era, local authorities wanted to have their powers restored and then to be left alone.

At the same time, the incoming government had its own expectations. Local government was viewed as providing some of the significant risks to its success and a second term of elected office in government. These risks ranged over a number of areas, including corruption, perceived inefficiency, and lack of responsiveness to the public. It was not surprising that after the long period of the Thatcher government, followed by Michael Heseltine's approach to bringing in business to solve local delivery issues, local government experienced low esteem. However, this was now a problem for a political party which was dominant in local political control and in charge of the national government too. The incoming government also had to operate within the same World Trade Organisation (WTO) and European Union (EU) requirements such as competition compliance for public services. Devolution was also an expected deliverable for Scotland and Wales. At the local level, each council had its own agenda which needed attention. The pressure to deliver improvements in education and social services had started to put a strain on other delivery areas. At the same time, smaller district councils, which had much less flexibility in their budgets, were continuing to face year-on-year reductions in their budgets and a consequent squeeze on their services.

There were also other issues to consider. Prior to the 1997 election, the economy had taken a positive turn and there was a strong commitment to maintain the conditions which had led to this position. However, retaining a tight budgetary approach was going to create tension in areas where there had been a continued lack of investment in 'public goods', notably transport infrastructure, schools, and hospitals as well as the rest of the public estate and realm. By 1997, Britain was also fully established as a multicultural society but it was clear that in some towns and cities, long-standing policies were leading to potentially inflammatory situations such as in Oldham and Bradford. There were also concerns about the police and their local accountability and management, not least as their annual requests for funds had to be passed on directly to council tax payers. These were all issues which had direct implications for local government, for expenditure and service delivery. The local authorities wanted to have a quiet life within a positive environment when this was unlikely to be the case.

The view of local government: the legacy of expectation

The legacy of this expectation was shared by local authority councillors and officers of all political parties. There were a number of key issues which an incoming Labour government would be expected to address. First, there was a concern at the degree of centralisation in the United Kingdom in comparison with other countries,

> In recent years, countries of Europe and North America have been forced to respond to local and regional pressure for decentralisation. Britain has been alone in proceeding down a strongly centralist path, not only under the current government but under most governments since the war. (Commission for Local Democracy 1995, p. 1)

It was also assumed that an incoming government would make a significant step change in working with the community in ways which were more democratically accountable. There was also expected to be a reduction in the provision of services by appointed quangos, which had accountability only to a minister, and for these to be returned to local democratic control. There had been long-standing concerns about the nature of appointments to quangos, which were frequently perceived as being made on the recommendation of the existing members of these bodies. As Greer and Hoggett (1996, p. 152) state, 'in this sense many bodies resemble self reproducing oligarchies which operate alongside government within a tacitly agreed framework which determines the criteria for eligibility for membership'. John Stewart (1996) has called this group of appointees the 'new magistracy'.

Quangos also gave rise to concerns about the lack of control and accountability in comparison with local authorities and their real powers. The utilisation of quangos by central government was seen to be a means by which local services could be controlled centrally. As Greer and Hoggett (1996, p. 154) state, the 'autonomy of local quangos is highly circumscribed', providing the opportunity for central control at the local level without local accountability. Finally there was a key concern that the variety of bodies set up to deliver services at the local level all had individual remits, which did not involve working with others at the local level. There was a sense that the ability to deliver single objectives in health and education for example could not be achieved without some change in this local organisational structure and there was an expectation that this would occur on the election of a new Labour government.

There were also concerns about the perceived lack of local authority powers in the United Kingdom in comparison with the rest of Europe. As Kitchin (1996) pointed out, local authorities in Britain have a different status from that given to local authorities in many other parts of Europe. Although this situation has always been the case, the ways in which local authorities operated until the 1972 local government reforms were seen to provide some local degree of choice in action. The decline in the status of local authorities to act in an autonomous way was seen to be most clearly represented by the reductions in freedoms to act in the choice of local expenditure. The erosion of these freedoms was seen to create a new relationship between local government and the central state. As Loughlin (1996) states,

> the recent reforms have altered the basic character of local government. The tradition of the self-sufficient, corporate authority which was vested with broad discretion to raise revenue and provide services has been directly challenged. Discretionary powers have been confined, structured and checked and the regime of local government finance is now such that it is virtually impossible for local authorities to diverge significantly from specifically centrally determined spending assessments. Local government has, in effect, been transformed from that of being the basic institution with responsibility for providing for those public services, no longer holds a necessarily pre-eminent status. (Loughlin 1996, p. 56)

Thus, the period post-1979 had led to local authorities being more restricted in their actions and having no general power of competence or duty to promote well-being in their own local authority area. By 1997 there had been a growing expectation in local authority organisations that this issue would be dealt with rapidly, particularly through the government's adoption of the European Charter of local self-government in the United Kingdom, which had already been signed by almost all other European countries. The signing of the charter in the United Kingdom was seen to be more than symbolic; it would represent a new status for local government within the state.

A further aspect of this issue was seen to be the attitude of Whitehall towards local government (Commission for Labour Democracy, CLD 1995). Whitehall distrusted the ability of local government to deliver and that there would be little improvement in the position of local government until these attitudes changed. As Jones and Travers (1996, p. 85) state, in reporting a survey that they undertook, 'Minister and civil servants have, in effect, played God with British local government'. They base this view on the reported 150 Acts of Parliament passed since 1979 which had a direct effect on the ways in which local authorities conducted their businesses. The survey produced a range of attitudes including one that the future role of local governance 'would be as "administrative holding companies"' (p. 93). The importance of these views also depended on each of the positions taken by individual departments. The Treasury's view about expenditure was seen to be critical as was the view of other big departments of state which worked directly with local government, relying on them for a great deal of their service delivery. The gap between some civil servants and local government is illustrated in the following analogy: 'the mundane nature of many local services appears to encourage (at least some) civil servants to believe that they possess: "Rolls Royce minds, while local government officers have motor cyclists minds"' (Jones and Travers 1996, p. 101).

The expectation was that, as a friend and supporter of local government, the post-1997 government would demonstrate a different set of attitudes, particularly through the generation of a new level of trust. In the incoming cabinet and ministerial team in 1997, many leading members had direct local government experience including David Blunkett in Sheffield and Hilary Armstrong, the minister for local government, who had experience in Durham County Council. Yet, there was evidence of concerns that local authorities had not been adequately self-reforming in their own approaches to governance and service improvement. In local government in the 1980s, the greatest impediments to reform and improvement were seen to be internal (McLaverty 1996). In 1997, there was an expectation in local government that change would be achieved by will and political control rather than any deeper consideration of a more fundamental need for change.

Notwithstanding the assumption that much of the change could occur within local government through internally self-managed processes, there was also an expectation that the constitutional basis for councils needed a major overhaul. In 1995, the CLD put forward proposals for a new style of council with both an assembly, comprising of all those who were democratically elected, and the executive, those who were taken from the elected number, to work directly with local authority staff to implement the programme for the area. The CLD, the New Local Government Network, and others also proposed that there should be a directly elected mayor or at least that the council leader position should be a full-time one. This was based on the perceived need to identify an individual who could be accountable as in U.S. and European models of local governance. The mayor of Barcelona, for example, was strongly credited for his role in regenerating the city. The CLD proposed both that the leader/mayor should have a range of principal tasks and should be the figurehead for the locality, more in line with the model in other parts of Europe. The kinds of tasks suggested were

- to prepare and submit a budget to the council
- to propose an annual policy review to the council
- to respond to the council scrutiny of the executive
- to produce an annual democracy plan including decentralisation to parishes, community councils, or in geographic areas
- to employ and oversee the officers and executive in implementing policies agreed with the council
- to exercise functions of the local authority
- to act as the representative head of the authority in all external events and lobbying. (CLD 1995, p. 21)

There was also an acknowledgement that other things would need to change including the role of councillors. There were concerns that councillors were spending too much time in meetings and not enough out on the patch (Audit Commission 1990). This was seen to be leading to a lack of trust and confidence in local government by individuals and communities. As Burgess et al. (2001, p. 30) state,

It is commonly asserted that local people

- do not understand who is responsible for delivering their local services
- are often confused about how councils make decision and see them as secretive and overly bureaucratic organisations
- consider that council decisions and the views of their elected representatives do not reflect their own priorities or those of their neighbourhoods
- perceive local authorities as wasting their money
- consider effects at 'consultation' as a means of post hoc rationalisation of predetermined decisions.

This perceived discontinuity between local councillors and their communities was seen to be linked to falling electoral turnout, but it was hard to see what any local council or political party was doing to address these concerns. Further, in some places, the main political parties could not find enough candidates to put up in each ward at local election, leaving some uncontested (Rallings et al. 1996). There was a clear concern about the democratic legitimacy of local government.

The concern of the 1997 New Labour government: the legacy of fear

At the same time that a huge weight of positive expectation was on the incoming government, the New Labour project also had great fears about local government.

Labour-controlled local authorities had been seen as one of the main causes of the party's failure to win successive elections in the 1980s and 1990s, and given the high number of labour-controlled local authorities in 1997, there was a fear that local government would be an Achilles' heel:

> There were plenty of people in the 1974 government who were brimming with new ideas on social policy and the no 10 Policy unit under Jim Callaghan's premiership tried to push these issues forward – for example on council house sales and standards in schools. But too often they foundered on the rock of Labour's unwillingness to offend entrenched interest within the party. (Mandelson and Liddle 1996, pp. 11–12)

Part of this fear had fuelled the process of rewriting the Labour Party's Constitution in 1995 to deal with the other party demon – the trades unions. Although the election of a government of a different party was seen to be a reflection of the need for change, there was also a sense in which the Labour Party reforms had made it a nationally electable party. The owners of the New Labour project would not want to see this undone at the first opportunity and to become a one-term Labour government.

There was also a sense in which the last Wilson and Callaghan governments in the 1970s had lost their way bedevilled by in-fighting, which had also been apparent in the immediate past Conservative Party in government. These concerns included some of the bigger issues such as the economy and Europe. Although the world was seen to be a different place post-1990, these were still present challenges to be faced.

There was also an understanding that these legacy concerns needed to be managed. In particular, there was an absolute expectation that privatisation of services would be stopped immediately. The failure to generate the understanding for these policies within a wider international and European trade agenda meant that there was a lack of understanding of the ability of any government to remove these policies which were opening public services to market competition. These were not easy matters to get over to a euphoric set of local authorities on the morning of 2 May 1997.

The incoming government's response to local government was unexpected and initially unwelcome across all political parties at the local level. The introduction of best value, already trailed before the 1997 election, was greeted with disbelief. The new government's concerns about other issues in local government – performance, community leadership, and transparency – were all stated in the local government white paper 'Modern Councils, Modern Services' (DETR 1998), being described as 'the old culture' (para. 1.10) and expressed as a continuing culture of paternalism from both councillors and officers towards the dealings they have with their communities. The second main concern of the new government with local government was local voter apathy, and the third was poor performance in delivery standards. The incoming government described this as an inward-looking culture in local government, which gave no priority to leading or serving its community. Further fears were also voiced in the white paper: 'Worse, such an inward looking culture can open the door to corruption and wrongdoing' (para. 1.11). This inward-looking culture was seen to be most easily expressed in the amount of time councillors were spending in meetings, whether these be open or behind closed doors where the public assumed rightly or wrongly that all the real decisions were taken. The future was described as one where 'councils everywhere should embrace the new culture of openness and . . . accountability' (para. 1.20).

Another major concern was the role of the press in influencing public agendas – a concern which continues. The press view of local government was not positive. The relationship between a newspaper's political standpoint and its influence on voting behaviour is difficult to understand although Gavin and Sanders (2003) have shown that it does have some effect. This may not only be through specific editorials or positions during general election campaigns but in the way economic events and conditions are reported. If the economy is going well, then there is an underlying positive mood to the reporting of economic news which makes it generally supportive of the *status quo* politically. When conditions are negative or giving case for potential concern, then the political backwash becomes more consistently negative which may have an influence on political opinions. This seems to suggest that the need to manage the media and the concentration on debates concerning 'spin' may be less important than the performance of the economy, with economic well-being scoring more positively than other factors such as political scandals or war.

One of the greatest concerns expressed by the new government was related to the public's perception of local government corruption. In a survey by Public Concern at Work undertaken in 1993 and quoted in the report of Commission for Local Democracy (1995), 63% of those asked were concerned about fraud and corruption in local government, although in practice this seems to be a much larger perception than reality:

> Asked about the source of their concern large percentage mentioned the media and local hearsay. Only a small number claimed that they had direct experience of fraud or corruption in local government. Of those, about one quarter said their concern was based on their working in, or with, local government. (Commission for Local Democracy 1995, p. 13)

Paving the way for reform

Given the expectations, the reforms appeared as a series of measures to resolve individual concerns. One of the main debates in the modernisation agenda has been whether there has been any coherence or underlying philosophy in the reforms. Apart from the challenges to change within the United Kingdom, there were also other major international drivers to 'reinvent government' (Osborne and Gaebler 1992). In some ways this was a continuation of the initiative to reduce federal control and increase state power which began under Reagan's presidency, but with a much greater emphasis on public value and public service ethos, which also was an underlying feature of the 1998 white paper. There was also growing evidence that a small government is more effective, efficient, and an emergent view that it was a pre-condition for a more robust economy. Within the EU, there was a continuing shift towards subsidiarity which was restated in the Maastricht Treaty of 1992, at the end of the U.K. presidency. These were important movements at a time when the Labour Party was reforming its approach following Tony Blair's election as leader. Any political party can be expected to look at these international trends not only to learn from another's experience but also to anticipate the change in conditions which may occur during their period in office.

Driving forces behind change? — entro -

Real issues on the agenda: which key issues did local authorities face in 1997?

Multicultural communities
The population of England had changed to one in which areas of most population concentration are more ethnically diverse. In the 2001 census, some 9% of England's population defined themselves as from a black or minority ethnic (BME) group. The extent to which multicultural issues have emerged has been shown to be related to the way in which local councils have approached them. Major civil disturbances in places such as Oldham revealed a long-standing policy of *de facto* segregation in housing and education. To this is added separate voluntary, cultural, and community groups which serve the needs of different communities. Cantle (2002) describes this as the development of communities with parallel lives with no contact between different communities.

Pressure for growth
Throughout the 1980s and the 1990s, the planning system had been under pressure, not only in the South East but also in other parts of the country. The pressure was caused typically by the demand for new housing on green field sites and also for edge of town development for retail and business park use. There had also been long-standing planning inquiries into airport growth for terminals and runways as this form of transport was growing through the new budget airlines which started to emerge at the latter end of the 1990s. This pressure had generated concern about the non-responsiveness of the planning system to provide for the demands being made of it. Within local authorities it became increasingly difficult to attract professional planning staff who were being offered more interesting and lucrative posts in the private sector to champion these schemes through the process. For local councillors, planning became a more politicised issued at the

ward level, where a councillor's ability to be re-elected could depend on the line which they took on a particular local development, whereas at council level, party political groups often removed the whip from planning decisions understanding that these were best determined locally. This inevitably led to some councillors being planning experts and for others to be totally disengaged from the process. The procedural side of planning meant that councillors had to understand much of the process and legalities of the system, which coupled with application site visits, and the high turnout in the public gallery often developed a sense of camaraderie in the committee members across the parties. As the planning system became more charged at the local level, the ability to determine a planning application within the 8-week period set in the national process became increasing difficult to meet. Both those in favour of developments and those against learned how to intervene in the process to some effect.

At the same time, the pressure for new housing development on green field land was giving rise to concern in many large cities. With a flight of the young, economically active residents often beyond their boundaries, fears for 'hollowed out' cities, which had already emerged in the United States began. Unless there was some rebalancing to utilise previously developed land and the investment in infrastructure which already existed, it seemed that the longer term prospects for cities would be bleak. The Heseltine initiatives in the early 1990s started to demonstrate that previously used urban sites could be used as if they were green field land – with large-scale master planning and development visions. The services in inner city local authorities – whether schools, public transport, or open spaces – needed to improve. The café culture which people were experiencing on holiday in North America or other parts of Europe needed to be introduced. Retail developments in the city centre needed to be as attractive as those outside. The structure of the house building industry which was strongly split between new build on green field sites and refurbishment companies needed to be addressed.

The opening phase of turning England from an anti-urban perspective began in earnest in the early 1990s, based on the kind of resurgence which had come through the remodelling of the Barcelona waterfront for the Olympic Games, and leading to Manchester making its own successful bid to host the Commonwealth Games in 2002 (Cochrane et al. 2002). Research studies on urban open space (Morphet 1990) and compulsory purchase orders started to identify the issues about how to move forward. The animation of place started to emerge as a new activity of town centre management. John Major's initiative to found the National Lottery also started to generate funding for heritage and sports projects which could improve older landmark buildings, restore parks, and create new sports facilities. By the mid-1990s, local authorities could see more readily how these approaches could be used to improve street quality, the attractiveness of their town centres, and the quality of life in their areas although it was not always possible to find the resources to do so.

Working in a 'joined-up' way with other public agencies

Although it is well understood that people often have a range of interlocking problems to deal with in their lives, the traditional response from the public sector has been to deal with these issues separately. From the early 1990s, there had been a switch in the policy emphasis within government, to promote 'joined-up government' (JUG). As Perri 6 et al. (1999, p. 16) describe it, 'The aim was to move away from organising budgets, targets, incentives, management structures and accountability around the administration of functions, towards achieving outcomes and finding solutions'.

The ability to focus on the customer rather than the organisation has now become a constant theme in public policy, with major public cases linked with failure to maintain a joined-up approach to data and information management. These cases range from failures in working with children in high-profile cases such as that of Victoria Climbie and the Soham murders to the case of an elderly couple dying after their gas supply had been cut off (Laming 2003; Bichard 2004). In all cases a more joined-up approach between agencies, sharing information, and common working practices have all been seen to be at the detriment of the victims. There are also concerns for the customer or citizen, often needing to report information several times over or having to provide slightly different information to a multiplicity of public agencies. In addition to the cases mentioned here, the most frequent outcome of this failure of agencies to join up is the difficulty faced by individuals and households to obtain their full entitlement particularly to financial benefits and, on the other hand, to manage fraud.

In addition to the benefits to the customer there are also some obvious savings in the administrative support for service delivery, with reductions in double entry of data into records, keeping them up to date, and also managing information relationships with other agencies. Perri 6 et al. (1999) summarise these benefits as follows:

For the public sector managers:

- Access to increased resources through pooling budgets
- Better management of turbulence
- Better balance of demand and supply through common points of consumer access and pooling budgets
- Savings in numbers of staff through co-location
- Reduction in 'dumping' of clients, problems, costs
- Flatter management structures
- Better understanding of the multidimensional nature of clients problems
- Improved communications networks
- Improving policy making procedures
- Greater managerial and political control over objectives set for professionals
- Greater trust between agencies and departments
- Recognition of common interest and need for long term relationships.

The gains for the consumers:

- Quicker and more comprehensive handling of cases
- Improved complaints procedures, satisfaction tracking and so on
- Higher quality of services. (pp. 19–20)

The primary means of attacking these issues of citizen barriers has been a variety of forms of JUG. In the Labour government 1997–2001, the focus on JUG came as a response to poor service delivery and the failure of the system to generate solutions around people rather than 'producer-driven silo delivery', where the providers of the service delivered to suit their requirements and did not join up with other departments or agencies. In 1997, the incoming government established Policy Action Teams (PATs) across a range of agencies to deal with major issues such as social exclusion. Another was the use of the Cabinet Office Policy and Innovation Unit (PIU) undertaking cross-cutting studies, for example, on *Better Policy Delivery and Design* (2001). Pollitt (2003, p. 35) offers a definition of JUG as the possibility of offering 'citizens seamless rather than fragmented access to a set of related services'. In this definition the other benefits are primarily seen to be producer driven, such as the achievement of efficiencies and reduction of negative impacts – all important but not necessarily as user driven in interpretation as many of the JUG initiatives suggest is their driving force. A further concern with definition remains that the citizen is still having to 'access' services rather than using JUG as a means of 'entitlement' – a move from citizen 'pull' in service delivery to government 'push', which would confirm a more citizen-centric approach.

The case for multi-agency and joined-up working appeared in a variety of ways. People were slipping through the nets of services while differential benefit and service rules meant that people continued to have difficulty accessing their full entitlement. The sense of this dislocation between agencies in the mid-1990s was seen to be considerable and it was an area which was identified for immediate change in 1997. Stoker (2004) demonstrated that fragmented approaches to specific performance targets in policy was leading to many local issues being ignored. Local authorities were able to take some steps to joint working through local relationships and the community commitments of those managing different agencies but these efforts at joined or coordinated service delivery for people or neighbourhoods were frequently achieved despite the system rather than because of it.

In health, the lack of funding at the local level meant that elderly people were being kept in hospitals rather than being discharged into community care or sheltered accommodation. The increasing costs of care and the numbers of older people in some localities meant that social services budgets were under considerable pressure which was exacerbated by the increasing local pressure to improve school performance. The nation became aware of 'bed blockers', older people who were kept in hospitals as there was no where else to go to. These kinds of issues contributed to longer NHS waiting lists and to the wider provision of health care. The system seemed to be intractable and the funding pressure was put under a further squeeze in the mid-1990s (Stoker 2004).

Performance

Although local authorities had been placed under increasing pressure to deliver against performance targets set by government, these were set for specific services and each had their own inspectorate, which expected that 'their' service was always the one which took priority. Targets and inspections were primarily geared towards a single focus rather than how much joined-up working contributed to performance improvement. For those in local authorities, it became an important objective to ensure that education and social service inspections occurred in different years if possible – not only because these inspections took a considerable amount of time and effort out of normal service delivery but also because it was impossible to have both social service and education at the top of the spending list in any authority in the same year, creating greater difficulty in obtaining a good score – or so it felt. There were also other inspectorates for benefits fraud and the Audit Commission which undertook a series of studies which illustrated the results of both good and poor practice.

Local authorities wanted this kind of regime to be removed. It felt as if all their priorities were being controlled by central government and there was also an increasing direction on expenditure. This had other consequences. At local elections, the voting pattern was either seen to reflect a judgement on central government's performance in some kind of overt understanding about the effects of this central control or people staying away from the polls. The morale of local government was low and there seemed to be little remaining energy to promote good performance despite specific schemes such as the Citizen's Charter which was introduced in the early 1990s as an attempt to deal with this issue.

Lack of confidence within local authorities

The political style of any council differs considerably, even between two local authorities which are run by the same party. Each council has an individual and distinct idiolect which needs to be understood by every officer of that council and anyone wishing to work with it. National party politics can give a lead to local policy, and it is often said that local elections are a judgement on the national party in power.

Even if voting is influenced in this way, party governance within any local authority can be very different despite party majorities. In the 1970s and 1980s, national party ideology was seen to be a central feature of the policy of some local authorities which either strongly agreed or disagreed with the government of the day. During that period issues such as the retention or demise of grammar schools, the implementation of privatised services, or the sale of council housing were also seen to be local expressions of national party political philosophy. This combination of party association between central and local policy had a significant impact on local authority confidence in the 1980s and 1990s.

The restructuring of local government in the period following 1991, with the introduction of the first unitary local authorities in England in 1995, was the first change since the reforms in 1974 and was seen as a significant step. It left the majority of the English population living within single-purpose authorities, but with most of the land area, that is, the rural population, living within a two-tier local government structure. The process which was used to pursue the implementation of unitary local government was one where local cases had to be made and supported by local people. This was inevitably seen as a costly and divisive process which emerged again when the issue of unitary governance was associated with the North East Regional Referendum in 2004.

Local authorities had also had a long period of time when they were hearing daily in the media that they were failing. There was a low expectation that any service improvement would be publicly acknowledged by communities or government. During this time, local authorities tended to progress the activities for which they had unequivocal responsibility, including environment regulation and street services. This unglamorous and essentially local end of service provision was seen to be the mainstay of council activity. Some local authorities were involved in a variety of regeneration programmes funded from Brussels and the whole drive to engage with the EU was often generated by the wish to find some additional funding to meet the needs of their localities.

Conclusions

The expectations on the morning of 2 May 1997 were high. For local government there was an overwhelming sense of relief that at last the long period of pressure and lack of confidence in local government would be over. The pressures to privatise services, sell off housing stock, and operate within a financial straightjacket would be removed. There was an expectation that the local would prevail over the central and that local government would be an area for quick and decisive action to 'set it free'. There was a fundamental expectation of sympathy and understanding. The delivery of these promises took much longer than anticipated but there has been a slow and steady movement to provide local authorities with freedoms and a more equal role with central government.

3

NEW APPROACHES TO DECISION MAKING IN LOCAL AUTHORITIES

Introduction: implementing local government reform

In May 1997, the minister for local government, Hilary Armstrong, former councillor in Durham County Council, introduced the measures which were to reshape local government in the coming years. The response to the perceived political risk presented by local government was immediate and pre-planned approaches were brought forward. Hilary Armstrong also recruited Beverley Hughes as her PPS, who was also the former leader of Trafford Council in Greater Manchester. Other senior local government colleagues with experience such as chief executives or chief officers were brought into the civil service and by 2006, there were three former local authority managers appointed as Permanent Secretaries of government departments, something that would not have been considered in 1997. This recruitment, which was initially *ad hoc,* led to the formation of the local government modernisation team in 2000 which was to help roll out the changes which were to follow (Morphet 2003a).

The programme to modernise local government was seen to be part of a wider constitutional reform agenda being pursued from 1997. Some of these reforms, such as devolution, had been long promised while the Labour Party had been in opposition and there was an immediate effort to move forward on these bills and subsequent referenda. Although the promises of devolution contained links with regionalisation in England, this was not seen to be such high priority as the outstanding promises to Scotland and Wales. England had to wait until the interim report of the Lyons Inquiry in 2006 before its own devolved settlement was outlined (Lyons 2006).

For local government, there was no doubt that this was to be a reformist agenda. As the 1998 white paper states:

> People need councils which serve them well. Councils need to listen to, lead and build up their local communities. We want to see councils working in partnership with others,

making their contribution to the achievement of our aims for improving people's quality of life.

   To do this, councils need to break free from old-fashioned practices and attitudes. There is a long and proud tradition of councils serving their communities. But the world and how we live today is very different from when our current systems of local government were established. There is no future in the old models of councils trying to plan and run most services. It does not provide the services which people want and cannot do so in today's world. Equally there is no future for councils which are inward looking – more concerned to maintain their structures and protect their vested interest than listening to their local people and leading their communities (*Modern Local Government: In Touch with the People*, Cmnd 4014 July 1998).

The programme of change commenced immediately in 1997 with the introduction of the 'best-value' approach to improving methods of performance management, initially through pilot programmes and then in all local authorities. When the legislation on best value was passed in 1999, it seemed more a legitimising formality rather than any indication of policy to come. The first formal indication of the scale of expected change in local government came in the white paper *Modern Local Government: In Touch with the People* (DETR Cmnd 4014), which was published in 1998. This covered the range of expected initiatives which were to follow in the Local Government Act 2000. Each council was to have its own written constitution and there was to be a new ethical framework. Each council was to separate the role of the executive from the rest of its functions. Since 1880, each council had operated a 'top-down' hierarchical model, with the power of the authority resting in the council and then being delegated to its committees and officers through a scheme of delegation. The new council was to be like a three-legged stool, with power being allocated to each of its three component parts and not providing the ability of any one of the three to exercise the powers of either of the other two parts. Thus, the individual roles of the council, the executive (whatever its form), and scrutiny were established.

The new council constitutions

The provision of a written constitution for every local authority in England represented a radical change in the approach to government and has passed into effect with little comment. As a requirement of Part II of the Local Government Act 2000, each local authority prepared and adopted a written constitution. The process of adoption was also new. The council could not choose its own constitution without recourse to the public's views on both its general form and the specific way in which its executive was to be established from the options available through the act, including a directly elected mayor. The constitution was required to be adopted for a 5-year period and was to be reviewed. The constitutions set out the respective responsibilities of each of the parts of the council and the way in which these parts interrelate. As with any constitution, or set of rules, it is in their use that the operational relationships come alive; nevertheless, the ability to develop a new constitution for a council and then to put it into operation is a significant achievement.

Before councils had written constitutions, they were required to have separate sets of operating rules – standing orders, a scheme of delegation, financial regulations, and contract standing orders. All of these operational rules were subject to regular review and in re-adoption at the annual meeting of the council usually held in May.

Electoral arrangements

As with many of the post-1997 reforms, the key questions had been a concern for ensuring transparency in decision making and involving the community in these processes. One of the key features of the new system was to be the increasing frequency of elections. Each local authority has the choice of whether to vote on an 'all-out' system every 4 years or whether to have elections by 'thirds', thus having elections 3 years out of every 4. There have been proponents for both systems. In the all-out system, it has been argued that the stability created by this time period generates the practical ability for the majority party to move forward on some key initiatives. On the other hand, this approach is seen to be more adversarial. Having an election every 4 years is also seen to be more likely to be tied to views on the success of the party in control in central government rather than being on local issues. The election by the 'thirds' system allows the electorate to pass a judgement on the council nearly every year and for local issues to be aired within campaigns. In the increasing number of councils with no overall political control, election by thirds provides the electorate with an opportunity to give one party the mandate although it can reduce the effective delivery time for major initiatives to the July–February period. This is the time available between settling new councillors and campaigning for the next election.

The second set of innovations concerned with the electoral arrangements related to the direct election of mayors. It was for any individual council to determine whether it would choose to have a directly elected mayor as the executive model. In some local authority areas, referenda were held following local petitions for the referenda, although not all referenda called in this way resulted in a mayoral model being adopted. Within those authorities choosing the mayor model, only one, Stoke, has the mayor/manager model which allocates the powers between these two posts. In the other examples, such as Lewisham, Newham, Doncaster, Middlesbrough, and Hartlepool, other patterns of power distribution have been established among the mayor, councillors, and officers.

The third was the move to experiment with a variety of voting procedures including all postal voting, other forms of voting using smart cards, web, and SMS messaging as e-voting pilots, together with voting on different days of the week. The variety of electoral pilots together with the scale of the electorate covered has led England to be seen as the electoral innovator of the world (www.politics.on.line.com). The United Kingdom now has the highest proportion of its population covered by various forms of voting than any other country. These initiatives have also been subject to research by the Electoral Reform Society (ERS), which has reviewed every process and outcome. In their report in 2003, the ERS indicated that all postal voting proved to be the most effective in increasing the turn out and this is now being increasingly favoured as an approach. However, there have also been concerns about the high levels of electoral fraud in some local authorities including Birmingham and Tower Hamlets.

The role of the council

In the new democratic arrangements for local authorities implemented after the Local Government Act 2000, the council was seen to have a different role. It moved from being the only source of power, which delegated its powers to others to act, to the part of the process which exercised specific roles and functions. Prior to the reforms introduced in 2000, the council was seen as the highest body of the local authority. It was required to confirm the actions of its committees, after agreeing which matters were delegated to them, and also to have major debates on key issues including the budget or a major local event such as a factory closure. The way in which council meetings operated in different local authorities varied. In some they were short and perfunctory, seen as merely a formal process which could be over in less than 30 min. In others, the council meeting was seen as the set piece event of each of the council's meeting cycles, where key issues could be subject to debate or decisions taken by committees could be referred for reconsideration and potentially a different decision. Council meetings are chaired by the mayor where a local authority has borough or city status. Elsewhere, the council is chaired by the council chairman. In the past, both the role of the mayor and the chairman have been seen to be non-political with a removal from party political affairs for the year of office.

The council post-2000 has responsibility for setting the budget and for approving specific defined plans. It is also the point of last resort for any dispute within the council. However, the power to act now resides with the executive. The form of the constitution selected by the council also allows for the council to experiment with the role of the full council meeting. In the Local Government Act 2000, the role of the council is now clearly defined. It is responsible for

- setting the budget
- setting overall policy
- the approval of specific plans which are defined
- dealing with referred decisions.

The council is also responsible for publishing the 'Forward Plan', which identifies the key decisions which are to be taken over the coming period. The form of the Forward Plan has to cover the following, although the precise presentation may vary at the local level:

- defining the key decisions
- compiling and agreeing the forward plan
- publish the forward plan
- reporting on significant executive decisions.

The scheme for the Forward Plan is also a matter of local determination. Thus, this might contain a financial trigger, with all reports involving expenditure over a certain amount being published and seen to be a 'key decision' and thus needing to be identified in the Forward Plan. The schema may also cover such issues as the impact on locality and there may be a link with the scrutiny process, where discussions on issues are covered before they are considered by the executive.

The council can neither transfer these responsibilities to the executive or to the overview and scrutiny function nor are these two areas of the council's activity able to transfer their functions to the council.

The changes after 2000 have provided an opportunity to create a variety of forms of council meeting with a series of innovations. In Leach et al. (2003) and the LGA (2003a) a number of initiatives are reported, including

- a state of the district debate (e.g. Salisbury, Arun, Shropshire County Council)
- ability to question any portfolio holder by any council member
- ability of any member of the public to question the executive (e.g. Camden, Lancashire County Council)
- hold single issue meetings (e.g. Carrick, Daventry, Thanet, Kirklees)
- webcasting meetings (e.g. Camden and West Lindsey).

The role of the executive

The role of the new executive within local authorities was seen to be at the heart of the reform of local government. The creation of a small and identifiable team, which could be enabled to take decisions without referring them to committees or officers was seen to be the cornerstone of establishing direct accountability to the community and electorate. Members of the executive were expected to be known in their communities. In the earlier system, decision making was seen to be a shared responsibility of the whole council. It was not possible for individual councillors, for example, to take executive decisions, a procedure which was seen to be a safeguard against corruption and to tie the whole council to the decision. The move towards individual or small councillor group decision making was instituted again as a means of overcoming corruption through openness. Added to this was the establishment of the scrutiny function to potentially examine every decision that is made. This separation of roles was perceived as critical, most notably for the accountability it would generate.

The role of the executive is clearly defined in the white paper and subsequent legislation in a way which had not been practiced before 1998. Although the Bains Report in 1972 proposed that each council should have a policy and resources committee, it was still a local decision of every council as to whether it should have such a committee and if so which powers it should be given. In the new constitutions, executives, regardless of their form, have been given clearer and unavoidable responsibilities which cannot be passed on to another part of the authority, even with the will of the council. In the white paper, the responsibilities of the executive were set out as follows:

1 Translate the wishes of the community into action
2 Request the authority and its community interests to the outside world
3 Build coalitions and work in partnership with all sectors of the community and bodies from outside the community, including business and public sectors
4 Ensure effective delivery of the programme on which it was elected
5 Prepare policy plans and proposals
6 Take decisions on resources and priorities
7 Draw up the annual budget including capital plans for submission to the full council. (para. 3.39)

The variety of forms of the new executive was the most complex part of the new constitutional arrangements for local government and could in some ways be seen to undermine their simplicity. Although providing local choice of the executive form, based on public consultation, the variety of options included in legislation were

• a directly elected mayor with a cabinet
• a cabinet with a leader
• a directly elected mayor with a council manager.

Even within these three options further varieties of approach emerged. First, within the leader and cabinet option the size of the executive was fixed at a maximum of 10. The range of powers given to each of the executive members in practice ranges from virtually no individual power to the ability to make sole decisions. In effect, many of the new constitutions veered towards the leader and cabinet model, within which decision taking was joint between the executive members of the cabinet. Very few local authorities have provided executive members with the power to make individual decisions. The other models have been slow to take off. Many councillors in district councils did not respond favourably to the proposed changes which they felt were for 'failing' councils and did not apply to them. Many councils campaigned for a 'fourth option' which would allow for the maintenance of a traditional committee system in smaller district councils. Many of the councils with the leader and cabinet model have created policy advisory committees, comprising of many of the non-executive members of the council, to advise individual executive portfolio holders. This has been deemed to be politically necessary at the local level and to overcome the sense of exclusion from decision making experienced by many individual councillors. As new councillors who are unfamiliar with the former system are elected, these practices may dwindle.

Proposals for further change were announced in 2006 when it was proposed that council leaders should be elected by direct or indirect election and that they should remain in post 4 years (DCLG 2006). This push to stronger leadership reinforces the view that stronger local leadership is more accountable to the local community. It also represents a shift back to the notion that 'all-out' elections every 4 years are preferable to elections by thirds, which was the prevailing view in 1997, when regular accountability was seen to be more important than strong leadership.

The emphasis on meetings in the town hall remains while the community leadership role has yet to be fully developed at the local level. Earlier studies of councillors have demonstrated that many stand for election to a council to join a second family. Spending more time in the wider community does not feed this particular need unless new means of creating standing leadership at the local level are generated.

Scrutiny and overview

If the council is to be held to account over its policies, performance, and delivery, the role of the scrutiny function is seen to be critical. For many elected councillors, the role of scrutiny seemed second best to that of being involved with committees where decisions were made, albeit that they may not have had a leading role in making these decisions. The popular view was that a scrutiny role meant being sidelined and being taken out of the process. It was up to each local authority to determine how the scrutiny process would fit into its own constitution and a wide variation exists. In some councils, the scrutiny committee has the power to call in decisions made by the executive while elsewhere they will concentrate on detailed reviews of existing or proposed policies. In some councils all decisions go to the scrutiny committee before they are taken for final decision. This range of practice is common in a newly emerging policy arena, and while it provides the ability of each local authority to use scrutiny in the way it prefers, this local discretion has also served to undermine its central contribution of holding authorities to account (Ashworth 2003).

In terms of scrutiny, only councillors who are not part of the executive can be members of any scrutiny process. The way in which scrutiny operates will also vary in each local authority (Sweeting and Ball 2002). Scrutiny is more likely to be used for other purposes including the quality of outcomes of earlier decisions, best-value reviews, or reviews cross-cutting the council.

For the new local authority constitutional arrangements which have been put into place since 2000, it is those of scrutiny and overview which seems to have attracted most research attention, perhaps because they were seen to be the most contentious to the majority of councillors before they were implemented. A review of good practice in overview and scrutiny conducted by Snape and Leach (2002) found that there were several key elements at the local level which included:

- The challenge of breaking away from traditional committee system
- The value of 'in-depth' studies of significant issues
- The value of more informal 'small group' (and individual) work
- The value of (selective) studies of external (or cross-cutting) issues
- Opening up the scrutiny process to their organisations and the public
- The value of pre-decision scrutiny of key decisions (via the forward plan)
- Ensuring that scrutiny is effectively (and directly) supported
- Developing a supportive senior officer culture
- Involvement in best value and performance monitoring – but on a selective basis
- Ensuring that work of overview and scrutiny is properly co-ordinated
- Developing a channel of communication between executive and scrutiny
- Preparing properly for 'select committee' and 'expert witness' type of work.

In effect, the issues which surrounded the introduction of the overview and scrutiny function remain in practice. It is often difficult to maintain the ability to consider issues without political party pressure and there can be a climate of distrust between the executive and scrutiny. Snape and Leach (2002) also describe this as the 'critical friend' dilemma. Leach et al. (2003) extend further their explanation of this issue:

> There are limits . . . to the extent to which multi-party leadership of overview and scrutiny can take place. Apart from full council meetings, they provide the main opportunity for opposition members – especially in a majority controlled council with a one party cabinet – to express their opposition. It is unrealistic to expect members who are not on the executive (whether of opposition or controlling parties) to conveniently forget their party principles and priorities when they enter a scrutiny meeting. The important issue is how they express those principles and priorities. The legitimate language of overview and scrutiny is the language of reasoned debate. Thus the challenge for an opposition member (or indeed a discomforted majority party member) is to channel their 'opposition' into an evidence-based critique of executive policy or decisions or an evidence-based argument for the adoption or modification of a policy. The appropriateness of this kind of challenge is one of the key assumptions which lies behind the operation of Select Committees in Parliament. (Leach et al. 2003, pp. 37–38)

In style, the scrutiny function is increasingly similar in function to the select committees in Parliament which also have a scrutiny role. These select committees were established in 1980 and since their introduction have now evolved in style.

As Ashworth (2003) points out, the relationship between the two models can highlight some of the weaknesses in the local authority scrutiny model such as the lack of centrally defined powers that scrutiny committees may exercise, their ability to have influence over resources, and their dependence on the support provided to them at the local level. Ashworth points out that in Parliament, MPs have considerable specialist support to undertake their work where this is much less likely to be the norm as yet at the local level. However, in her research, Ashworth found that councillors within scrutiny committees indeed did have confidence in their powers, which represents a change in the initial views reported by Leach et al. (2003) and Snape and Leach (2002).

One perceived weakness in the parliamentary system is seen to be the desire of those serving on select committees to be members of the administration and therefore not to be seen to be too critical of the executive through these means. Although they may have been true in the past, the second term of the Labour government has served to demonstrate that there are some MPs who see their career to be in the chairmanship of such committees, for example, Gwyneth Dunwoody in Transport and Dr Tony Wright in Public Administration. The chairmanships have also become places for former ministers to take the lead although there is still some 'to-ing and fro-ing' with the executive. However, the profile of the parliamentary select committees has been high at times when the official opposition has been weaker, but to be criticised by members of one's own party can be more difficult to sweep aside than to be criticised by the opposition.

Scrutiny is seen as a way of improving the 'user voice' in local government (Wright and Ngao 2004) although it is not the only mode available. Nevertheless, the routine inclusion of a scrutiny function into local government may take some time to mature as it has in Parliament, and much of the response to scrutiny still remains negative (Johnson and Hatter n.d.). The future for local government scrutiny seems secure, with a national scrutiny centre now established at the University of Greenwich. At this centre, copies of all scrutiny reports in local government are held while training courses for those supporting scrutiny in local government and in Parliament are offered jointly.

The emerging roles of local councillors

A further major element of the new system is the amount of financial support which can be given directly to elected members for positions of responsibility. The scheme and the amounts will vary in each local authority, as will the definition of posts of responsibility. In some councils, the elected mayor receives the equivalent of a salary whereas in some district councils, the responsibility allowances are set at lower levels. At the upper end of these arrangements, the new approach shows that being a council leader or mayor is the equivalent of a full-time job and needs to be recognised as such. As yet the provisions for the equivalence of redundancy arrangements which apply to MPS if they lose an election are not yet available but this might be a consequence for elected mayors or leaders appointed for a 4-year term as proposed in 2006 (DCLG 2006). Many councils have instigated independent reviews to consider the levels of the allowances paid to councillors based on the level of work they are asked to undertake. In some cases this has led to a job description for councillors being prepared such as in London.

Other movements towards describing councillors as 'employed' have also occurred. In Wales and Scotland, for example, councillors are being offered retirement packages to encourage older members to stand down although they have not been adopted by most councils. A further development has been the use of the provisions of employment law, including the utilisation of the Council of Tribunals to cover issues related to councillors' standards issues.

The key features which determine the roles of councillors are still the same. The party organisation at the local level decides who receives which post and what role a Councillor has to play. In councils with small majorities, there may be considerable negotiation about who receives particular posts and the extent of executive power over specific defined decisions. The old system had built up a sense of camaraderie within committees particularly where in some councils it was traditional for councillors to stay with one committee for the whole of their local government career. Elsewhere it was and is common for councillors interested in specific issues that are less popular with others, such as planning to develop a sense of community based in part from the banter between members which grows up in any council as people meet often – twice or more per week.

These new arrangements have also provided a legitimate space for those members who have a life-long interest in a particular issue that might be libraries, care for the elderly, or the needs of young people. In the former system, they were often respected but did not always have an opportunity to be more proactive in putting forward proposals for action. The post-2000 system has provided greater opportunity for these members in a variety of ways including being a portfolio holder for youth or the elderly, for leading a scrutiny review of library policy, or by being able to run debates at open council meetings.

The new constitutional arrangements for local authorities suggested that there would be more transparency in decision making, with fewer decisions being taken in 'smoke-filled back rooms' prior to open committees. This is the stuff of politics at any level including Parliament, but the principle of airing issues surrounding a decision (albeit previously rehearsed) or the opportunity to question assumptions or objectives through the scrutiny process are intended to make this more transparent. This has placed more of the council's work in the open.

The extended roles and changes in responsibilities have resulted in councillors being given more support. Typically now a councillor will have a PC at home with access to council documents and correspondence. Each councillor will normally have a ward surgery on a regular basis although this may be less common in rural areas where councillors are more well known and accessible within their communities. The new roles also require more development and training and in areas such as standards and planning these are now required. Some councils have developed accredited training packages for their councillors although the take-up of such opportunities still varies considerably at the local level.

All of these changes still leave room for conflict based on either politics or difference of opinion and in some councils this may be more institutionalised than in others. In the past, the approach taken within any particular council was part of its own culture and way of doing things. However, these approaches are now less a matter of local choice as the Audit Commission's performance management processes examine the extent to which internal relations between councillors and between councillors and officers are functional and add to the well-being of the area. A change of councillors and/or party control at the time of an election can provide a natural point to evaluate and adjust the way in which a council operates. This may be more difficult where political control changes less frequently, leading to ossification or where the political control is on a knife edge over a long period of time. It is also important to remember that any organisation, regardless of its function, develops a way of working to get things done – changing the key personnel or a structure does not always change the underlying culture of progressing business, particularly if the organisation is large and not engaged on issues that have not attracted the concern of the centre. Some service areas also have traditionally attracted very little political involvement and the new systems will not automatically address these.

The legacy of the 2000 Act changes has not yet fully matured in local authorities and more changes will emerge in time. What is clear is that the recommendations of the Widdicombe Review (1986), which strongly discouraged the provision of full-time councillors employed by other councils, has been reinforced but has been replaced by the recognition that local politics requires full-time leadership in a way that has only been partly acknowledged before. Councillors with leading roles should be 'paid' by the authorities. What remains to be seen is whether councillors, who act as local leaders or elected mayors, will still see these roles as a stepping stone to Parliament or will see their roles at local level to be more powerful.

Reforming local government representation at the centre

The scale of local authorities has a significant bearing on their functions and roles. In metropolitan, unitary, and London borough councils, the authorities are said to be 'unitary', that is, they have responsibility for all the council functions within their area. Most people in England live in unitary authority areas. Elsewhere, councils have their functions divided. County councils are responsible for children, adult services, libraries, and trading standards together with some planning, waste and transport functions, although this latter group is set to be transferred to regional arrangements of some kind in due course. District councils deal with benefits, environmental health, planning, housing (where this is still a main service), refuse collection, and street cleaning. The district council provides more of the uniform services and county councils' more age-specific services but these lines are often blurred in practice through a variety of local initiatives. Both county and district councils have direct elections for councillors and these areas have two elected members at least, one at each level in each area, with some councils having multi-member wards.

Before 1996, each type of local authority had its own association, that is, the County Councils Association (ACC), the Association of Metropolitan Authorities (AMA), and the Association of District Councils (ADC). The creation of the LGA was seen to be a means of strengthening and unifying local government's voice with central government. In the earlier period, much of the lobbying and advice work was undertaken by local authorities coordinated by the associations. The LGA has a greater reliance on its own staff to develop policy and liaise with central government in a more day-to-day way. The county councils have retained a County Councils Network (CCN) which operates from within the LGA head-quarters with their chief executives and other leading officers retaining separate meetings.

In the period since 2000, there has been a newer grouping of local authorities dependent on their performance. The introduction of Comprehensive Performance Assessment (CPA) in 2002 has led to councils being grouped into five categories regardless of their size – excellent, good, fair, weak, and poor. Those local authorities which are excellent have 'freedom' from inspections and other plan returns whereas those which are weak have a greater provision of specific support, help, and capacity building from a variety of local and central government sources. The introduction of these league tables has had a variety of effects particularly on staff who may choose to leave a failing or weak council if their skills are in demand elsewhere. In other councils, there is a move to attract leading staff to deal with problems such as the advertisement for the chief executive of North East Lincolnshire (30 April 2004 LGC) which had a strap line – 'it can't get any worse'. Excellent councils are now grouped in an Innovation Forum which has developed new ways of working. Such groupings are emerging as a significant determinant of the way in which councils view each other. These approaches to excellence have also had a significant impact on the way in which local authorities have approached central government. In the past, repeated failure was often dealt with, some might say rewarded, by additional funding to deal with ailing schools or high crime rates. The approach now differs and it is excellent and good authorities are rewarded whereas weak and failing councils attract much more detailed scrutiny. These excellent councils also now have a strong voice with government in proposing new ways of working.

Thus, local authorities view the issues which they face through a variety of lenses and may seek to present the issues and challenges which confront them in different ways depending on the audience.

Conclusions

The reform of local government decision making and accountability has been significant and in the future, the year 2000 will be viewed as a major watershed representing these changes. In a time of other constitutional reforms, the changes in local government have not attracted as much interest as other areas and have remained unsung (Toynbee 2004). As yet these reforms are still working their way through the system and there may be a further round of change when each council's written constitution is reviewed.

4

PROMOTING WELL-BEING AND THE COMMUNITY'S INTEREST

Introduction

One of the longest standing discussions within local government over the last century has been the extent to which its dependency on specific legal powers erodes local government's role in delivery and its ability to lead and serve its communities. The absence of a written constitution in the United Kingdom unlike almost all other countries, has meant that the role of local government has not been enshrined as a tier of government. This is usually expressed as local government's lack of a 'general power of competence', that is, the ability to act without ensuring specific powers or '*vires*' are available. Much legal discussion has arisen about these powers and their limitations, particularly when local authorities have been faced with new and difficult situations such as an economic recession in the locality. The interpretation of this approach has always meant that the ability of local authorities to act and spend has been limited.

The implications for local authorities have been significant in other ways. Successive governments have seen the ability to control local authority action as entirely appropriate. They have argued that local authorities are an extension of the administration of government, delivering at the local level what is required by central government. This approach has been seen to reduce the standing and independence of local government and has created the following problems:

1 reducing the democratic mandate of the locality elected politicians;
2 potentially reducing the electoral turnout – why vote for an administration which has no power;
3 maintaining the economic dependency on government not least in terms of the proportions of funding being provided from taxation rather than from locally generated revenue;
4 making the United Kingdom one of the most centralised countries in the world.

There are also counter arguments to this. Local authorities have a huge degree of freedom within these overall legal constraints, which accounts for differing levels of performance. The argument advanced before the 1997 election, that local government could be the Achilles' heel of new Labour, stems from this root. In order to deal with this issue, two approaches have been developed which are at opposite ends of the spectrum in this debate about the need for a more independent status for local government. There have been moves to create tighter controls on local authorities through the rigid application of targets and spending direction, with far fewer degrees of local freedom. This approach has been for local education programme which, over successive years, has generated more centralised and uniform targets and at the same time has dictated the means by which these targets are to be achieved.

This practice has now been taken forward by other government departments who have seen their services suffer as a consequence of the push towards education spending. The Department of Health then required secure levels of expenditure and leadership for adult services and the Department for Transport, which had been a loser to the other big two departments, started to adopt this approach for transport expenditure.

This process seemed to have no end, until 2003, when it became clear that there were serious problems being generated by this approach. The first was that local authorities could no longer meet the education budget as set out from the funding they had been given. This led to both an internal investigation and to a broader review of the reasons for an unduly high increase in council tax levels for 2003–2004 (Audit Commission 2003d). The outcome of the study not only led to more funding being found but also to a greater focus on the review of local government finance (the Lyons Inquiry 2007).

A second response to this increasing control was introduced in 2000 in the provision of the power of well-being in the Local Government Act which was then coupled with the introduction of 'freedoms and flexibilities' for excellent councils (ODPM 2004l). This approach was designed both to change central government's approach to local government and to help local authorities act independently. This chapter reviews the way in which the local authority power to promote economic, social, and environmental well-being creates the potential for the use by local authorities of 'implied' powers (DCA 2003a), that is, allowing a freedom to act without recourse to more specific legislation and how these powers are being brought into use through their application in the generation of Community Strategies.

Understanding the role of a general power of competence – the European Charter of Local Self-governance

Local authorities in the United Kingdom had long been disappointed by successive governments' refusal to sign the European Charter of Local Self-government. Although the charter does not express complete freedom to act on the part of local authorities, it had a symbolic place in the struggle between central and local government in the 1980s and the 1990s. The European Charter of Local Self-government was established under the auspices of the Council of Europe, came into force in September 1988, and was adopted by the United Kingdom in 1997. It requires that countries which have ratified it to comply with certain conditions, principles, and practices:

1 *Self-government.* All local authorities should be responsible for managing a substantial proportion of public affairs in the interests of the local population.
2 *Legitimacy.* The powers of local authorities must be recognised in legislation, or better still in a constitution.
3 *Application.* The rights apply first and foremost to local authorities, but may also apply to regional authorities where such authorities exist.
4 *Powers and responsibilities.* Local authorities must be able to act freely within legal limits, on all matters that they are best placed to deal with because of their closeness to ordinary people. These powers may be delegated. Local authorities must also be consulted on any matters directly affecting them but outside the direct scope of their own powers.
5 *Actors.* Local elected representatives, with appropriate training and financial compensation, will carry out their democratic duties.
6 *Method of implementation.* To carry out the tasks entrusted to them by the electorate, local authorities must have executive bodies and be able to recruit the necessary staff.
7 *Resources.* Financial resources should be made available to local authorities to enable them to carry out their tasks. Resources may be collected by local authorities in the form of taxes or grants. Provision must be made to distribute resources evenly and protect financially weaker local authorities.
8 *Monitoring.* The activities of local authorities are supervised to ensure compliance with the law, not to assess the expediency of the decisions taken.
9 *Protection of local self-government.* Local authorities must be able to go to court to defend their interests.
10 *Cooperation.* Local authorities must be able to cooperate with other local authorities within the same country and, where provided by law, with their counterparts in other countries.
11 *Boundaries.* No local authority boundary can be changed without prior consultation of the local community concerned. (Council of Europe, 1985)

Once the U.K. government finally signed the charter, the principles contained within it have been taken forward in a number of ways, notably through the Local Government Act 2000, although the first principle of 'self-government' has yet to be fully realised.

The duty to promote the economic, social, and environmental well-being of the communities being served

One of the legacies of local government being a 'creature of statute' was the long-standing principles of *vires* and *ultra vires* in local government. It was always necessary to identify which legal power supported any action. The body of legislation covering local government is large and frequently local authorities utilised different powers to undertake the same action. Some councils regarded specific actions as being *ultra vires*, that is, without powers whereas others believed that there were legal powers which would enable them to act. Legal boundaries led to many authorities taking a constrained view of the actions which they could undertake and in some authorities, councillors would limit actions to 'statutory duties' to minimise expenditure. In 2001, over one-third of local authorities in England were 'debt free' and were limiting their ability to provide discretionary services. The imposition of a duty on local authorities to promote the well-being of their areas changed this position. Additionally, this power has given local authorities 'implied' powers to act which did not exist before (DCA 2003a).

A proposal to promote the economic, social, and environmental well-being of a local authority area was first stated in the 1998 White Paper on local government (DETR 1998). The new proposed duty was expected to be allied with a power for local authorities to enter more easily into partnership working and for them to be able to take any action in support of their community provided that it did not contravene any specific legal requirement not to act. (The government stated its intention to maintain a reserve power for reasons of national security). The power was included in the Local Government Act 2000 and came into immediate effect. The expectation was that the utilisation of this power would be demonstrated through the local authority's Community Strategy (DTLR 2001a), which was a new requirement for all local authorities in England contained in the Local Government Act 2000. The Community Strategy is a statement of the community's needs and objectives and how they are to be met in a multi-agency way, as represented by the LSP, a new non-statutory local body also established in 2000.

LSPs have continued to develop with their roles enhanced over time. They were given a central role in the creation of LAAs in 2004 and are seen to be the way forward for public service reform initiatives (ODPM 2005e). In 2006, it was proposed that local authorities should have a duty to prepare an LAA with the LSP (DCLG 2006). The Community Strategy has been left to develop at the local level until 2006 when it was proposed that it become a Sustainable Community Strategy (DCLG 2006) and has a more formal role as the plan (and programme) for each local authority. All of these approaches also sit within the Lyons Inquiry's proposals for 'place shaping', which reconfirms the leadership role of local authorities in their areas (Lyons 2006). The final element of the development of a more integrated approach to public sector programmes and delivery at the local level is the proposed duty of public bodies to cooperate (DCLG 2006).

Since the duty of well-being has been imposed on local authorities, it is hard to point to any specific changes which have come about. Various pleas to local authorities to identify powers which are further restricting their actions, which the secretary of state is also able to deal with under a specific power in the Local Government Act 2000, have by and large failed to come forward (DCLG 2006).

The duty of well-being is intended to promote the notion of community leadership within the area, joining with other public agencies, the private and voluntary sectors through the LSP.

The contribution of local authorities in the generation of economic well-being was recognised in the Treasury's Review of *Productivity in the UK: The Local Dimension*, published in 2003 and ODPM, HMT, DTI (2003). This concludes that the local contribution to national performance is critical, whilst intra-regional variation in economic performance is greater than inter-regional comparisons. The assumption has been that the differences between regions and localities had been due to inherent economic weaknesses in these places, that is, to macroeconomic factors. However, research undertaken for the National Productivity Review demonstrated that neighbouring local authority areas with much the same conditions have significant differences in terms of productivity performance. The Treasury, therefore, concluded that economic performance in part is not a 'given' and that it is susceptible to local action.

Another area where the duty of well-being is intended to operate is in working with other agencies. The ability to focus on the customer or 'front line' rather than the organisation or 'producer' has now become a constant theme in public policy, with major public cases linked with failure to establish and maintain a 'joined-up' approach to data and information management (Bichard 2004). In their advice on data sharing, the Department for Constitutional Affairs (2003a) used the duty to promote well-being from the Local Government Act 2000 as one of the main means through which local authorities can achieve this joined-up approach within their own organisations and between other public agencies.

Promoting community leadership

The ability of local authorities to work with the local business community, health, and the voluntary sector vary significantly according to local need and priority. In the public sector, the mass of separate targets between agencies has been one of the significant hurdles of joint working. As the democratically elected representative, politicians (central and local) have acted as the quasi-customer (Foster and Plowden 1996), to represent their choices. It is the essence of a political party that it stands for a group of 'preferences' in this sense. The same may be seen as true in relationships between politicians and citizens. However, politicians represent a wide range of interests in their communities.

The interaction between the state and the citizen has become more complex, with inter-linked and sometimes unexpected consequences. This has led to a shifting view. In order to inform decision making, councillors have to understand the likely or real impacts of their decisions at the local level. Have all the expected outcomes and consequences been understood at the point of decision and will they have the desired effect? At the same time, local politicians elected for 4 years may not be able to agree on positions on a variety of issues before they take office. The future choices or indeed challenges are simply 'unknowable' in that sense. A political tradition that represents a view which does not see the relationship with the community as one of constant interaction is now likely to be seen as distant and uninformed. It is, therefore, more difficult for politicians to act as quasi-consumers and citizens in a general sense and politicians now need to represent a range of community views increasingly based on evidence from various sources rather than one where an elected representative 'knows best' and makes decisions on the basis of a 4-year mandate without any further interaction with the locality.

In some localities there has been significant resistance to working with community groups or seeking the public's views, as this approach has been seen to undermine the elected councillor's democratic authority. Gyford (1991) argues that this has been a consequence of increased politicisation of local authorities. The community development movement, started in the 1960s, has demonstrated that some communities need to be encouraged to put forward their views and need new skills to be heard. These approaches have been developed through neighbourhood renewal and housing stock transfers, where increasingly neighbourhood participation in decision making has been a growing success story (e.g. Knox and Alcock 2002; Taylor 2002).

A variety of methods of consultation have now been introduced including surveys, focus groups, and citizen's juries which are seen to offer a more deliberative tool to citizen-based decision making rather than traditional representative approaches (Wintour 2003). These means of including citizen's views during decision making are seen to be part of a move away from 'aggregative' or 'vote-centric' models of democracy (Goodin and Niemeyer 2003) to ones which recognise the longer process of idea and policy formation as part of the formal consultation rather than formal decision taking.

Citizens' juries have been used by a number of authorities to contribute to decision making on key policy issues (Smith and Wales 2000; Wakeford 2002). Much like a court, citizens' juries are selected to represent the community as a whole; they receive evidence and then they take a decision on their preferences. As with any jury, members of the selected group can be swayed by arguments of those giving evidence or indeed through debate with other members of the jury. Like other methods of deliberative participation, citizens' juries demonstrate the complexity of issues which have traditionally been refined before they have been presented for decision making. The process demonstrates that a number of alternative solutions are possible and there may also be various formulations of the problem being considered. These processes can occur through the policy development phase 'within' policy communities and the political process (Goodin and Niemeyer 2003), but these more citizen-based approaches both expose that chain of debate and demonstrate more clearly the range of options. In some methods, such as agenda setting through round tabling, the process provides a means through which opinions can be 'rounded' through discussion. Those with very specific views that can be polarising and go unchallenged in more traditional methods such as public meetings can be the subject of peer challenge during these processes. A similar outcome can be delivered through phone-ins and threaded web discussions or blogs.

In active forms of participation, there is an assumption that a citizen has to have some reason to engage in these debates in the first place (Goodin and Niemeyer 2003) whereas approaches such as surveys can attract views that will be less subject to shared debate. As shown in research on the involvement of younger people in political processes, it is often the interest of someone else that leads people to participate actively. People attend a meeting or a demonstration with someone else for whom this issue is of high salience or use new means such as mobile phone messaging (Macintosh et al. 2003). The use of citizens' juries have attempted to overcome this in that jury members can be approached randomly through the electoral roll or selected in a stratified way by a commercial polling organisation.

There have also been other ways of encouraging citizens and communities to more actively participate in decision-making processes between elections. Some have involved debate such as the establishment of single-issue council meetings or questions times. There has also been webcasting council of meetings that have included not only the main council meetings but also, in Camden, the executive and planning and licensing meetings where there is public interest in the decisions (LGA 2003c). These debates have been available both live and as recorded video inserts in the council web site. West Lindsey and Lancashire County Council have also webcast their meetings with the latter's executive meetings attracting over 500 viewers during the year, when public attendance at such meetings would normally be minimal or non-existent. Others have established civic fora encouraging more debate such as the Greater London Authority's London Civic Forum (www.londoncivicforum.org.uk). At these, both individuals and group representatives attend sessions, 'having a voice' in debate in order to influence decisions, although the forum is not specific about how this is achieved. These approaches may be more readily categorised as councils communicating with their citizens rather than actively engaging them in decision making, but they are seen to be opening up the process.

No matter what new means of engaging citizens in decision making are employed, some argue that this will still not convince communities that local government makes a difference. Quoting a senior official at a No. 10 seminar on new approaches to governance, Wintour (2003, p. 11) writes, 'if you want to reconnect people with local politics in poor communities, you close down all the crack houses, you arrest the criminals and bang them up for a long time, and people will say thank god local politics is working for once'.

Community engagement has sometimes gone much further such as in housing and area-based regeneration and area-based 'zones' which were introduced in the first period of the Labour government 1997–2001, including health action zones (HAZs), education action zones (EAZs), and employment zones. Some of the main concerns about these place based regeneration and improvement have been associated with the potential disconnect between the improvement of place and the communities that are served by these improvements. On the one hand, some have argued that improvement in place leads to rising land values and subsequent social displacement of those people in need. On the other hand, social inclusion programmes which seek to improve skill and education attainment levels without improving the locality, lead to people moving away. As McGregor et al. (2003) indicate, this is a very difficult set of initiatives to hold together and a continuing tension, but the research identified more mutually reinforcing policy processes on the ground which included

- overlapping board membership
- joint strategy meetings
- greater operational integration
- ,capturing and sharing tangible benefits.

McGregor et al. (2003) also identified the ways in which these initiatives could be brought closer together by action from central government. These were to

- become more joined up at the centre and require this down the line
- give flexibility to local delivery to promote effective working
- set joined targets and make organisations jointly responsible for meeting them
- drive joint working down through national organisations
- create more stability
- make integration a key programme design and redesign component.

Some commentators argue that community participation processes are creating new ways of working. Wainwright shows that localities such as Luton and East Manchester are not only working within the governance system but also developing new 'bargaining' powers. Bargaining is seen to be a variant of workplace relationships where participation confers legitimacy on the process and is therefore sought in the many layers of government. Its inclusion also adds legitimation to the politicians and officials who are involved with ensuing delivery. This participation creates a more equal position for the community although it may be more difficult to retain its independence.

There has also been recent research on changing British attitudes to civic engagement through the establishment of a citizen audit (Pattie et al. 2003; Pattie and Johnston 2005). This found that people still have a high notion of 'civic duty' in that they generally support obedience to law and also engage in at least some civic activities such as participation in groups. Pattie et al. found that 55% of people are engaged in at least one group, with some in more. In addition, one in two people support the community in an informal way and one in three belong to informal networks.

Community Strategies

The duty placed on each local authority in England to prepare a Community Strategy (s. 1a, Local Government Act 2000), has been little discussed, which is surprising given its potential strength. The importance of the Community Strategy as the 'plan of plans' and its role in the consequent reduction of other plan requirements on local government have been mentioned as part of the general context of the modernisation of local government and its implications for planning (see Allmendinger et al. 2003a; Morphet 2004a). It is clear that Community Strategies are growing in importance in the forthcoming processes of perform-ance and outcome delivery expected of local authorities in the period 2005–2008 through CPA. Community Strategies are also at the heart of the LAAs (Audit Commission 2004a), LPSAs (LGA 2004; ODPM 2005a), and LSP consultation.

Given the many concerns about the potential variety of targets and approaches at the local level, the 1998 Local Government White Paper proposed that each local authority in England should prepare a community plan or strategy which would help to bring some coherence to the approaches to dealing with local problems from a variety of agencies. This is to be 'a clear and understandable strategy for every area, based on an analysis of the area's need and priorities for future action' (para. 8.13). This Community Strategy was seen to have a key role in being a 'bidding' document to central government and to other agencies, for example, the lottery or Regional Development Agencies and also to provide coherence to other plans which are developed locally, with a health example being cited in the white paper. This is also linked with the review of area-based initia-tives (ABIs) and the plethora of funding streams for which local authorities are required to bid (ODPM 2003d; Audit Commission 2004a).

The preparation of a Community Strategy has attracted little attention, although the majority of local authorities have either published or are in the process of doing so. Recent developments in the role of the new Sustainable Community Strategy (SCS) (ODPM 2005a) suggest that it is to play a core role in 2008–2012. Unlike some of the other local authority plans, Community Strategies are not required to be set within strictly determined frameworks but rather to be prepared 'with regard' (s. 3) to guidance published by government, the first of which was available in December 2000, shortly after the act passed into law (DTLR 2001a). The duty to prepare a Community Strategy rests on all local authorities, regardless of their tier.

Community Strategies were expected to contribute towards the achievement of better local coordination between local public bodies which serve localities, to help these agencies be responsive to the needs and concerns of people, to help agencies to deliver services in ways which suit them, and to take into account future generations, incorporating sustainability. The proposals contained in the Community Strategy are expected to allow local communities to articulate their aspirations, needs, and priorities; to coordinate actions of the council and other organisations which operate locally; to focus action on the future and also to achieve sustainable development, including the consideration of regional, national, and global aims. The guidance also states that the Community Strategy should have four key components – a long-term vision, an action plan identifying shorter term priorities and outcomes for the area, a shared commitment for action, and arrangements for monitoring, implementing, and reviewing the strategy with a provision to ensure that communities are updated on the delivery of the strategy. They are increasingly 'evidence based'.

Community Strategies vary in their presentation. In *20:20 Vision*, the Community Strategy for Redditch (Redditch Partnership 2003), the key issues identified by the community are set out alongside the actions proposed by the partnership, together with the ways in which success will be measured. In comparison, the Staffordshire Community Strategy sets out the community's requirement listing below how they will be achieved. There are no measures of success indicated in the document (Staffordshire County Council, n.d.). Many are vision documents with the key needs and aspirations of their communities set out together with a generalised programme of delivery. Some have set their horizons to 2020, taking a longer term view of the future of their localities. This broader approach may lead to a greater convergence in style in due course as Community Strategies begin to play a more central role in the relationship between local authorities and the government in their central accountability processes. At present these can be expected in two main areas – CAA and LAAs.

In many ways, the Community Strategy is more similar to an EU local European Social Fund or Leader 2 programme than perhaps any other local authority programming document which is in current use. With its focus on needs, it suggests a more evidence-based approach to establishing policy and yet community preferences still have to be incorporated. The Community Strategy also has a coordinating role with other bodies and brings it closer to the functions of the LSPs. The proposals to develop the role of the Community Strategy into the Sustainable Community Strategy (DCLG 2006) will also serve to increase the 'programme' role that it has. This also mirrors trends in the EU to promote 'territorial cohesion' which represents a wider approach than hitherto to dealing with spatial inequalities through their funding programmes with the earlier 'structural funds' taking a more pinpointed approach in localities and regions. Territorial Cohesion, like SCS in England, applies to the whole of the EU's area.

Community leadership and CPA

The introduction of CPA for each local authority was a significant change in the method of performance assessment for local authorities. It was based on performance judgements provided by the existing range of inspectorates and an assessment of the local authority's community leadership. Local authorities were critical of the methodology for a variety of reasons but in general there was a concern that the CPA process did not concentrate adequately on responses which local authorities developed to support their communities and to promote well-being. It was also felt that the experiences of citizens and users of services were not truly incorporated into the judgements which, on the whole, were seen to be weighted towards centralised rather than local objectives. In the CPA process post-2005, the Audit Commission (2004a) methodology has been altered to lead on locality and on the local authority's leadership role in the community as expressed by the LSP. In its co-ordinating role, the Community Strategy becomes a focus for this process. From 2009, CPA will be replaced by CAA.

Community Strategies and Local Agenda 21 (LA21): towards environmental well-being

Community Strategies are required to take into account regional, national, European, and global issues. The creation of Community Strategies has stimulated a debate on how to balance the social, economic, and environmental requirements, some of which are expressed in other plans. This is a particularly difficult issue for work on promoting local sustainability, which has been developing since the Rio Earth Summit in 1992, and always took the social, environmental, and economic issues of sustainability to be at its core (Tuxworth 2001).

More recently in the United Kingdom, sustainability has been interpreted in a more qualified way as 'environmental sustainability', although some would still prefer to use the wider definition. When local authority interest in LA21 was stimulated in 1992, this coincided with local authorities wanting to assert their powers in the context of a hostile government. There was inevitably some concern when guidance on the preparation of Community Sstrategies (DTLR 2000) identified that it was intended to incorporate LA21 statements (Pinfield and Saunders 2000). This has also led to a widely held belief among sustainable development practitioners 'that LA21 has been effectively subsumed by Community Strategies within Government's own policy agenda' (Lucas et al. 2003, p. 5). These fears might have been justified were it not for the requirement that all local authority plans and proposals need to be the subject of Strategic Environmental Assessment following the implementation of the European Directive (ODPM 2004h). Although there are some who regret the merging of LA21 into the wider agenda, there is also a view amongst others that there are strengths to be gained from drawing together LA21 with Community Strategies. One of the main issues is to ensure that the development of LA21 approaches since 1992 is not lost as the wider agenda is pursued and there is now some evidence of the abandonment of standalone LA21 (Lucas et al. 2003).

However, local authorities are still seen to be at the forefront of leading local sustainable practice as the Stern (2006) and Eddington (2007) reviews of climate change and transport, respectively, demonstrate. Local authority controls over planning, transport, and waste management are seen to be fundamental in helping the United Kingdom meet its climate change obligations. These issues have been reinforced through the 'place-shaping' agenda (Lyons 2006).

Community Strategies and Local Development Frameworks (LDFs)

The duty on each local authority to develop a Community Strategy to be the 'plan of plans' leading to the reduction of the number of plans required has been supported by the coordination of those plans which remain. For land use planning, development plans have a much longer history and for many years have acted as the only overarching plan in the local authority which has had a legal basis although local authorities may have undertaken the preparation of corporate plans for their own purposes. The development planning processes have a specific legal character which also set them apart from some of the other plans as do the process of adoption through a public inquiry process before a Planning Inspector.

In 2000, as local authorities were given a duty to prepare a Community Strategy, the reform of the planning system including the development plan process was also underway and was set out in the green paper on planning (DTLR 2001b). This green paper proposed that LDFs should be adopted in place of the current development plan process and that these LDFs would provide a spatial expression of Community Strategies. As a means of providing guidance on this relationship, ODPM commissioned research by Entec (2003) and issued a draft – Planning Policy Statement 12: Local Development Frameworks (ODPM 2003c). Entec's research which was in the form of guidance suggested that it is necessary to develop an 'effective' relationship between the two approaches:

1 A clear strategic framework for the future of an area and for sustainable development is provided for the general public.
2 One strategy does not undermine the other.
3 The policy content of the two strategies is consistent.
4 The processes are co-radiated and opportunities are taken to share resources.
5 Linkages are made to other policy areas which help to deliver objectives: principles of co-operation, information sharing and exchange and communication are followed in working on the respective strategies. (Entec 2003, p. iii)

This research also suggested other policy and process linkages including such issues as common branding for consultation. This is particularly important given that the LDF has to be accompanied by a Statement of Community Involvement. Entec also suggests that Area Action Planning could be viewed as a shared process between the Community Strategy and LDF. Despite this advice and guidance, there is little evidence that these processes are being undertaken together even if they are being prepared within the same time frame. It is as yet unclear how this relationship will emerge over time although it is apparent that the two processes will draw closer over time.

Removing plan requirements

Although much of the process of local government reform since 1997 has been seen as being increasing the burden for plan submission, s. 6 of the Local Government Act 2000 also gave the power to the secretary of state to remove legislation that was not needed. Further, in the local government white paper, *Strong Local Leadership – Quality Public Services* (DTLR 2001c), there was a commitment to reduce plan requirements of local authorities. This has been followed through with a consultation paper on *Removing Plan Requirements* (ODPM 2003l). Proposals are made to remove seven plans. In addition, the consultation stated that the DfES proposed to remove most statutory education plan requirements and replace them with a single plan, with the exception of those authorities judged to be of the highest performance level in education who will not need to submit at all.

As these proposals to remove plan requirements take effect, central government departments which 'own' these plans are providing guidance to local authorities about how to integrate their existing requirements into the Community Strategy. One example of this is the draft guidance on integrating cultural and community strategies (Creative Cultures 2004). Cultural strategies were established as a requirement of local authorities (DCMS 2000) and covered the range of activities which are the responsibility of the DCMS, including parks, performing arts, museums, film, tourism, and play. The guidance on integrating the cultural strategies within the Community Strategy recognises that there is a common set of interests based on well-being, which incorporate the cultural life and diversity of any locality.

Conclusions

Although there have been problems joining up and developing a coherent approach to a locality and its people, there is some coherence emerging between the Sustainable Community Strategy and the processes which go into developing it. In the CPA process post-2005, the Audit Commission (2004a) proposed that the methodology be altered to lead on locality and to attempt a better balance between local and central targets. It was also proposed that there should be a greater focus on the local authority's leadership role in the community as expressed by the LSP. Some excellent authorities also suggested that the LSPs should develop Local Public Services Boards which bring together all public services in a more formal way (ODPM/Innovation Forum 2003; LGA 2004). This has led to the establishment of LAAs across English local authorities, with operational spending programmes. In future, these LAAs may develop 'special purpose vehicles' (DCLG 2006) or organisations to create new structures of joint public sector delivery at both the local and city levels, the latter through MAAs.

Some local authorities have also established public service boards (e.g. Kent County Council and Swindon) to formalise a joint public sector delivery budget and programme.

The future for the well-being of the people, businesses, and neighbourhoods of any area is increasingly seen as a common public sector task. It may take some time for cultural change to follow policy intention but if the government continues to reinforce this integration, then, in time, new ways of working together at the local level will emerge which will potentially be more citizen focused and more efficient.

5

PERFORMANCE AND FREEDOMS

Introduction

Concerns about local authority performance in 1997 were derived from research on public perceptions of poor performance and non-delivery of local authorities. The drive to improve local public services including health, education, and transport has been extended to include crime and anti-social behaviour. The local authority performance agenda has become increasingly critical to central government as the greater part of local government funding is derived from national taxation, so the implied link between local and central government performance is made. Further, local elections have increasingly been seen as a judgement on the party in national government rather than as a response to local issues and political choices.

The creation of an improvement and performance agenda for local governance is not new although it increased during the period 1979–1997, when the Conservative government considered that local level funding would be wasted as part of the major philosophical differences between the local and central state. During this period of decline in central government confidence and the circumscription of freedom to act, local authorities explored new ways in which to develop their roles such as LA21 for local sustainable development practices and other environmental services (Morphet 1993b).

In 1997, local government anticipated this pressure on performance to be lifted. There was an expectation that there would be a reduction in performance regimes, an increase in discretion on local funding priorities, and the removal of requirements to expose services to competition. However, local authorities severely underestimated the lack of confidence in their delivery and democratic performance. The government's first move was to introduce the best-value (BV) regime, which measured detailed service performance and still included the requirement to compare costs competitively. This replaced the requirements of Compulsory Competitive Tendering (CCT) and retained a requirement that services should be subject to competition for delivery from third party providers. This was received with considerable hostility by local authorities.

Notwithstanding this immediate move to introduce the BV regime, the local government minister did promise that improved performance by local authorities would lead to increased freedoms and flexibilities. At the time, this promise was viewed with scepticism by local authorities.

Although concerns remain about the extent to which Whitehall will 'let go', there is evidence that new approaches are developing which will lead to potentially more freedom at the local level. These include

- the local authority's duty to promote the well-being of their area (Local Government Act 2000)
- the power to trade
- raise charges and freedom to borrow (Local Government Act 2003)
- the reduction in submitted plan requirements
- the review of inspection arrangements
- the introduction of the Best Value 'lite' process. (ODPM 2003a)

The Local Government Act 2003 also introduced CPA processes which have taken the lead in drawing together all the assessment processes at the local level and placed each local authority in a league table. Not only have these been controversial but are also transitional as after 2008, Local Service Inspection (LSI) will develop a more joined-up way of reviewing the performance of local public service providers and has been accompanied by a review of local government finance, a 10-year review of local government and the introduction of LAAs (ODPM 2004k).

This chapter outlines the development of these approaches and the overall journey which links performance to freedom. It is a work in progress, and thus it is possible to see counter trends and contradictory actions during this process. Not all Whitehall Departments have the same confidence in local government.

The role of the Audit Commission

The main assessment of local authority performance is undertaken by the Audit Commission, which was established in 1983 and works within the requirements of the 1998 Audit Commission Act, a combination of earlier legislation. The Audit Commission is appointed by central government which also appoints the chair and the individual commissioners. It operates separately from government. Although government sets the terms of its work and, in part, its outcomes, the Audit Commission sets its own way of working and publishes its own findings. The Audit Commission is responsible for reviewing and scrutinising the work of local government, health, and the police. It also works jointly with other government inspectorates including Ofsted. As a mark of its independence, the Audit

Commission has always been self-funded, although since 1998 it has approximately 15% of its budget funded by central government in recognition of its work in BV and establishing the Housing Inspectorate (Kelly 2003). A similar role for central government and its bodies is undertaken by the National Audit Office (NAO), which publishes reports and works with the Public Accounts Committee and the Select Committee system of scrutiny in Parliament. In 2004, the Audit Commission announced its first major study with the NAO, where the organisations jointly reviewed health and IT.

The role played by the Audit Commission is seen to be significant, authoritative, and influential. It has also changed over time. As Kelly (2003) indicates, the Audit Commission has not been afraid of tackling difficult or controversial issues and being critical of governance. After many years of debate, the Audit Commission undertook a review to see whether proposed increases in council tax were owing to a lack of control in local authority costs or whether the extra burdens expressed though council tax had been caused by additional government burdens which had not been fully funded (Audit Commission 2003d). The study found that although local government could be more efficient, many of the financial pressures experienced by local authorities were generated by central government adding 'new burdens' without associated funding. This report marked a turning point in the balance of power in the central/local relations debate, which had previously always been led by central government being critical of local government performance. Instead, central government was seen to be more silo driven in its policy and delivery demands.

The report led to two major changes. The first was a fundamental review of local government finance, and the second was an assessment of all new burdens with a cost of £100,000 or more to local government as a whole (i.e. not per authority) and is employed across all central government activities which are expected to affect local government including service and performance changes, policy, and legislation. Before this, local authorities were expected to 'prove' that they were being given new burdens by central government in an annual round of negotiation, but ultimately these figures were always aggregated and were representative rather than specific.

Best value: why competition?

The notion of 'best value' had been associated with competition by Michael Heseltine in the early 1990s, and in Mandelson's and Liddle's book *The Blair Revolution* published in 1996. In this, they stated that there was

> a requirement to recognise that there are circumstances in which local councils are much better at planning, financing and regulating public services than they generally are at owning, managing and directly providing them. There may be clear exceptions to this, but, in general, good management requires flexibility and freedom of action which rule-bound

local authorities are not always good at providing. This has been recognised by Labour in its policy that not every local service has to be carried out by the local council, and that councils should be allowed how to choose how best to get the job done – directly, through formal contracts with private operators, or through partnership with voluntary bodies and other organisations. The important thing is to ensure the highest quality, the most responsive service and the *best value* for money. (Mandelson and Liddle 1996, p. 151; emphasis author's)

The best-value process

The BV process was introduced in 1998 and the Local Government Act 1999 provided its legal basis. The process has six stages for each local authority:

1 Establishing local authority-wide objectives and performance measures.
2 Agreeing a programme of fundamental performance reviews to be set out in a local performance plan (LPP).
3 Undertake performance reviews in key areas of council expenditure and across all services.
4 Set and publish efficiency targets in the LPP.
5 Subject to processes of independent audit and inspection and subsequent certification.
6 Refer areas requiring intervention to the Secretary of State.

The new range of national performance indicators which were drawn up in 1999 were expected to demonstrate performance over a range of key areas including strategic objectives

- cost and efficiency
- effectiveness
- quality
- fair access.

Councils were expected to set performance targets to meet improved delivery over a 5-year period. As part of this, councils were expected to aim their service objectives, delivery, and performance targets to ensure that they reached the top quartile of councils. In terms of the four principles for defining BV, each of the '4 Cs' – challenge, compete, consult and compare – had its own objectives. First, the requirement to pursue challenge was to ensure that a particular service was justified and that the way it is being delivered is the most appropriate in the circumstances. This could include delivering a service in new ways with technology or with other service partners. In terms of 'compare', local authorities were expected to bench-mark their performance with both other local authorities and providers including local businesses in order to establish whether costs were comparable. In achieving the need to consult, councils were asked to ensure that they could demonstrate that the local people had been asked about the quality and effectiveness of service delivery whether they were direct recipients or just local council tax payers.

Finally, local authorities were asked to demonstrate that services are delivered in a way which can be demonstrated to be financially competitive, that is, that they have investigated a variety of means of competition. All these processes, together with an assessment of the previous year's progress, were to be brought together in an LPP, which was made subject to local consultation.

A BV inspectorate (BVI) was established, under the ambit of the Audit Commission and BV inspectors were specifically trained and drawn from senior officials in the local government and other public services.

There were initial significant concerns expressed over the cost and time of BV. Both of these issues were internal to the organisation and the additional costs also included payment to the BVI to undertake the reviews. There were also concerns initially about the delays between stages of the inspection process and the length of time taken for receiving feedback. Concern was expressed in many councils about the cost of funding this additional layer of inspection together with the perceived quality of many of those recruited to undertake the task. Where inspectors were deemed to be good, it was said that this was because the BVI was recruiting the best talent away from local government thus making it difficult for local authorities to maintain or improve their service delivery. The reports of the BV inspectors, who were initially overwhelmed by the volume of work, were often late and the results often seemed initially inexplicable to many councils.

Many council chief executives and senior officers had concerns about the quality of the inspectors who were being used and their familiarity with the type of authority being inspected, for example, unitary or district, and also concerning their knowledge of the service which they were inspecting (Kelly 2003). These concerns were obviously part of the setting-up process and in part were to be expected, although there are those who would argue that the speed in setting up the process lead to some of these problems in delivery. There was also a sense in which the process was seen almost to be non-negotiable – the authority was a 'justified' recipient of criticism rather than have some reasonable points to make. A second set of costs related to the payment required for the council's external auditors to assess the data quality and integrity of the BV performance indicator evidence which also added to each council's audit fees.

In the first two or three years of its implementation, the BV process was developed into a smoother practice and in 2002 the establishment of the CPA process – the 'league tables' for local authorities was announced. The review of the BVI led to a merger between the BVI and the Audit Commission's District Audit services to create a more joined approach to BV and value for more money auditing (VFM) at the local level. By 2003, BV reviews and inspections had become a more regular feature of performance review inside local authorities. The initial approaches of a templated methodology had softened to allow more local choice on which services are brought together and on the process. By 2003, the focus had also moved to the contribution of BV into the CPA process, as one of its key components, but by no means the only determinant in assessing a council's performance.

Over time it is clear that the BV process is now emerging as a critical tool in local performance review. In particular, research into the timing and nature of reviews has shown that the process can demonstrate its contribution to the improvement process. In a series of 10 case studies of organisational change resulting from BV reviews (Entwistle et al. 2003) it was found that BV has contributed to improvements in activities ranging from recycling, library services, and local tax collection. The main findings of the research were that, as shown below, there are some pre-conditions for improved service delivery, which the BV process has helped to encourage:

1   Good reviews lead to change, that is, that the process is not a waste of time.
2   Inspection empowers the BV regime, that is, it adds weight to the process so that even a poor review could still lead to change.
3   Reform is not rocket science – it still depends on four main types of activity – partnership, service redefinition, process reengineering, and centralisation/decentralisation of delivery.
4   Much of the impetus to change comes from challenge, compare, and consult rather than competition.
5   BV works with other drivers for change.
6   Change takes time and money – including good project management (and rushed reforms can lead to failure).
7   Leadership counts – from a small group – a lack of ownership leads to poor reviews.
8   BV needs realistic member involvement.
9   Scoping matters, that is, there must be support from chief officers to support radical reform and not be too narrowly focused.
10 A corporate approach is key.

BV requirements also applied in Wales. However, the Welsh Assembly Government decided that it wished to move to a more tailored system which it considered better met the needs in Wales. The Wales Programme for Improvement (WPI; WLGA 2003) was established. The decision to 'abolish' BV in Wales was seen to be difficult to understand, but the announcement foreshadowed the introduction of the CPA regime in England only a few weeks later.

After nearly 10 years of operation, BV has been clearly embedded within local authorities. The inspections have become part of the Audit Commission processes. Many councils now receive 'lighter touch' inspections and the process of reviewing BV inspection reports has been taken into the scrutiny function in the new constitutional arrangements.

Comprehensive Performance Assessment (CPA)

The introduction of the CPA process arose following discussions about further progress in local government in 2001. The two overarching concerns were the need to reduce the inspection and target burdens on local authorities and to increase freedoms and flexibilities which were promised by the then local government minister in 1997. These freedoms would be allowed to councils which were deemed to be 'excellent'.

The white paper on local government *Local Leadership: Quality Public Services* was published in December 2001 and heralded the new performance regime and implemented in 2002. Once all single tier and county authorities had been through the process, it was reviewed, *CPA – The Way Forward* which was published by the Audit Commission in 2003 (Audit Commission 2003b). Although most of this paper is concerned with details of how councils move between the five divisions – what are the mechanisms and the means – the statement of key principles for the future is important in the way it shows the expected direction for future local government in England. The key objectives are as follows:

1 The judgement needs to better reflect the experience of the citizen or user of services in the locality.
2 Within the CPA framework of performance, there needs to be full recognition of the 'shared priorities' for local government agreed by the Central Local Partnership.
3 CPA needs to measure the influence and impact of a council in its locality – fulfilling its community leadership role with the Local Strategic partnership when working with other partners, agencies and organisations to lever higher-quality public services for all.
4 CPA needs to measure performance against both national and local priorities providing an appropriate balance between the two.
5 CPA needs to be aligned with existing performance frameworks, including national and local public service agreements, and neighbourhood renewal floor targets.
6 The impact of deprivation, diversity and spending on council performance needs to be reviewed and further consideration given to how these issues are included in the framework.
7 CPA needs to measure the cost effectiveness and value for money delivered by councils. (Box A Audit Commission 2003b)

The inspection role of the Audit Commission is now seen to take precedence over the role of advice on ways to improve services, in 'an inspection for improvement paradigm' (Davis et al. 2004). At the same time, the process of the CPA has moved to be one which is more centrally related, not to the performance of individual services as represented in the BV approach, but on what the council and its partnerships are achieving for the area. In December 2004, the new approach to Corporate Assessment as part of the CPA process was published (Audit Commission 2004a), which clearly represents this change in emphasis through the themes and questions which the process will pursue through its key lines of enquiry (KLOE). These are

• What are the ambitions for the community and its areas?
• Are these prioritised and is there a strategy to achieve delivery?

- What is the council's capacity to delivery?
- What is the council's performance management system?

Does performance assessment work?

The performance assessment framework for local authorities is one of the major changes in culture since 1997 and has been a continual process of change in the subsequent period. There is now pressure on local government to take on more of this performance assessment role within the authority and in local public services in general (Raynsford 2004).

There are signs that this is having an effect on the overall performance of the local government. The LGA has accepted a challenge target that all local authorities will be excellent or good by 2008 and is working to achieve this task with local government. Research has also shown that specific ways of assisting councils which are classified as needing to improve their performance have been effective. One model has used political mentors to assist poorly performing councils in the recovery process, although no one approach is seen to be adequate on its own. In a study of the approach, Whiteman (2004) also shows that some politicians are anti-pathetical to being mentored and he comments on the lack of support for local councillors from national parties. Other work demonstrates that each council has its own performance improvement and recovery cycle, which may not work at the same rate and demonstrates the complexity of the achievement of improvement in performance in an individual council. Hughes et al. (2004) show that the degree of acceptance of the process, the perceived boundaries for action, and the overall financial position of local authorities are all important components for this process. Additionally, the CPA recovery plan can be seen as a distraction from improving the basic services in some local authorities.

The future of inspection may be for a lighter touch and more systematic performance monitoring approach through business monitoring tools. There is also considerable potential for greater unification in inspection regimes. Whilst these remain separate, they bring additional costs to the process and retain the risk of competing, and in some cases, contradictory service objectives being set. This process is being discussed through the Inspection Forum although local authorities might express the view that progress has been limited, with the traditional service divides being replicated in CPA processes, which were meant to offer a more joined-up process. However, the role of inspection is set to continue as it has provided some evidence that it works to improve performance. The study on Inspection for Improvement (OPSR 2004) undertaken by the Office of Public Service Reform for the Cabinet Office and the Treasury demonstrates that despite the need for further change on the process of inspection, above all it has assisted in improving customer delivery in public services. One of the key ways in which these processes are being developed is through the twin approach of national standards with devolved and local discretion in their delivery to achieve outcomes – inspection should be of outcomes and not of inputs.

In the development of a greater integration of the inspection processes which are experienced by local government, OPSR has proposed some principles of inspection and external review, which each inspectorate should be able to demonstrate in detail. These are as follows:

1 The *purpose* of improvement. There should be an explicit concern on the part of the inspectors to contribute to the improvement of the service being inspected. This should guide the focus, method, reporting and follow-up of inspection. In framing recommendations, an inspector should recognise good performance and address any failure appropriately. Inspection should aim to generate data and intelligence that enable departments more quickly to calibrate the progress of reform in their sectors and make appropriate adjustments.

2 A *focus on outcomes*, which means considering service delivery to end users of the services rather than concentrating on internal management arrangements.

3 A *user perspective*. Inspection should be delivered with a clear focus on the experience for those for whom the service is provided, as well as on internal management arrangements. Inspection should encourage innovation and diversity and not be solely compliance-based.

4 *Proportionate to risk.* Over time, inspectors should modify the extent of future inspection according to the quality of performance by the service provider. For example, good performers should undergo less inspection, so that resources are concentrated on areas of greatest risk.

5 Inspectors should encourage rigorous *self-assessment* by managers. Inspectors should challenge the outcomes of managers' self-assessments, take them into account in the Inspection process, and provide a comparative benchmark.

6 Inspectors should use *impartial evidence.* Evidence whether quantitative or qualitative should be validated and credible.

7 Inspectors should disclose the *criteria* they use to form judgements.

8 Inspectors should be *open* about their processes, willing to take any complaints seriously and be able to demonstrate a robust quality assurance process.

9 Inspectors should have regard to *value for money*, their own included.

10 Inspectors should *continually learn* from experience in order to become increasingly effective. This can be done by assessing their own impact on the service provider's ability to improve and by sharing best practice with other inspectors. (OPSR 2004, p. 34)

Intervention

The principle of intervention in those councils which are found to be failing has been with local government since 1997 but seldom used in a formal way. The first candidate for intervention was the LB of Hackney on the basis of successive reports by the District Audit Service. The next group of councils deemed to be in need to help were the failing councils identified in the CPA league tables, which included Hull. The next group of poor councils were announced in December 2003 with Plymouth this time being declared as being the poorest.

For those councils which are deemed to be poor, an approach to helping them improve performance has been delivered through a range of means including the appointment of a lead official, usually a former local authority chief executive, and a package of assistance both in the form of some financial support and from consultants appointed by Central Government who could help develop local capacity and improvement.

There has as yet been little research of the factors leading to a council failing but there are some which seem to be common to councils in this group. These factors include poor relationship between councillors and officers, which may involve mistrust and possibly bullying. There is also often a failure to support the role of the head of the Paid Service, that is, the chief executive in bringing together the officers within the council to support delivery. In these cases, individual councillors and some officers may have been pursuing independent objectives in a competitive and highly politicised way, which may also reflect factionalism within the majority party. As in other organisations, tension within the 'family', in this case a majority political group, can be far more destructive than any competition between political parties. Some of these failing councils have been new unitary councils, that is, Hull, Plymouth, and Swindon that were often different and dominant within their former county. The establishment of these new unitary councils did not provide the means to consider a more radical change unlike East Riding and Herefordshire which were based on new boundaries. This was a perceived handicap but ultimately proved an advantage in the creation of a new council.

In the 1998 White Paper, one of the options identified for intervention was the potential to put services out to the private sector. This may have encouraged a number of councils expecting to be designated as weak or failing to move to the provision of services with a major strategic service partner (although this is not the only group of councils moving in this direction). As yet, there is no research as to whether such an approach makes any real difference to delivery in these cases, although Hughes et al. (2004) found that

> outsourcing provides a possible opportunity to bring in external management expertise. Effective outsourcing, however, requires good client skills. Where recovering authorities lack these skills they run the risk of poor contract/partnership management and opportunistic behaviour by contractors. (Hughes et al. 2004, p. 73)

In some cases individual services have failed in councils, including Hackney and Lambeth, where privatisation was used to deal with an already failing service. The need to ensure a service is running well before it is outsourced has not always been recognised. A second issue is a weaker council's ability to maximise the benefit an external provider can bring in terms of skills and service improvements. Third, many of these contracts were established in the expectation that additional work would be attracted, a key selling factor to the local trades union community. Although some of this has occurred in Middlesbrough, this is still not generally the case.

The final act of intervention, where the Secretary of State directly takes on the running of a local authority, has yet to occur, although the action in Hull has been the closest. Councils can change and improve over time. What makes an excellent council? This research has yet to be done but it does not seem to rest on any obvious factors such as party control, locality, or deprivation. What does seem to come through is a sense of being in control of what is happening and not being the victim of fate. The ability to understand what is going on in schools, in service delivery, and taking forward the interests of the community for everyone all seem to be significant factors. Beyond this there are difficult issues of reputation management. The ability of a council to work with to all its key partners and to deliver on the promises in an open way seems to be a particular trait. Another is to ensure that the council is well known to all the different parts of government, to be in established dialogues, and to create an early warning link should there be any problems. Finally, this knowledge of interest and triumphs at the local level leads to ministerial visits and to invitations to participate in pilots, pathfinders, and trailblazers of emerging national initiatives all of which are seen to be performance-enhancing activities.

Capacity for delivery

One of the major concerns has been the ability of staff within local government to meet these challenges and the morale of local authority staff, particularly when working in councils that are not performing well. Concerns have also been expressed about the introduction of a 'transfer' market – good officers being attracted to lower performing authorities in order to improve them. It has also been recognised that there is a need to ensure that local authorities are able to attract the right numbers of staff and deploy them appropriately. Last, there have been concerns about the ability of local government to continue to attract the calibre of staff it needs to manage these complex issues.

These issues have been brought together through the preparation of a Pay and Workforce Strategy for local government published by ODPM and the Local Authority Employers Organisation (ODPM/EO 2003). This strategy looks at five key areas:

- Developing leadership capacity
- Developing the skills and capacity of the workforce
- Developing the organisation
- Resourcing local government
- Pay and rewards.

The Joint Strategy indicates the importance of ensuring that these issues are developed within the context of devolved decision making but also within a framework of national targets and policies could so that overall delivery is not undermined. In addition to the needs of the workforce is also it recognised that the capacity and skills of the elected members in each local authority need to be improved.

In looking at workforce issues in local government, the Audit Commission has undertaken a study to identify why those working in local government leave (Audit Commission 2002). They found that the key factors were

- Bureaucracy and paperwork
- Lack of resources
- Workload/hours
- Not valued by government
- Pace of change
- Not valued by managers
- Not valued by public
- Pay
- Career progression
- Line manager
- Autonomy.

There are also factors which attract people to work in local government which include

- Working environment
- Job satisfaction
- Convenient working hours
- Convenient location
- Promotion prospects
- Job security
- Organisational culture. (ODPM/EO 2003)

There also seem to be some clear differences between working in local government and in the private sector which are set out in the Workforce Strategy (ODPM/EO 2003). The benefits of local government employment are seen to be pension provision, length of working week, sick pay, and flexible working arrangements. In comparison, local authority employees are rarely seen to receive the benefits provision of the private sector including free or subsidised cars, healthcare, or performance-related pay, although this may now be converging.

Freedoms and flexibilities

For authorities looking for the delivery of more freedoms and flexibilities this has seen to be slow in delivery. Those authorities in the top CPA category of 'excellent' have had some immediate relief from plan submissions. These authorities have also joined the Innovation Forum where new ways of working are being developed. More generally the power to promote well-being has not been seen as providing many more opportunities. A further raft of 'freedoms' was also delivered in the Local Government Act 2003. These freedoms fell into two main categories – the freedom to trade and the freedom from some of the financial controls placed on local government, particularly around capital financing. The freedom to trade and to levy charges for some services provided a return of the type of powers which local authorities had prior to the introduction of CCT. The Act also gave councils the ability to engage in business improvement schemes and to provide rate relief for small businesses. In addition to these new means of using and generating local funding, councils are also being given an incentive to encourage more business start-up and movement by being allowed to keep some of the additional revenue levied on the business rate from new businesses.

Conclusions

Since 1997 central government has considerably expanded the performance framework of local authorities. This is in response both to fears about the performance of local authorities in 1997 and to increased delivery pressure on individual ministers who have imposed increasing targets on local authorities to meet requirements placed on them by the Treasury. Some of the targets have been seen to work whereas others have produced unintended consequences. The most frequent complaints relate to the disassociated nature of government performance targets and the definitions used in their assessment. There is some expectation that this position will be improved post-2009, when a common public sector performance framework will be implemented although the extent of change will depend on individual ministerial targets set in the 2007 Spending Review by the Treasury.

6

DELIVERY WITH PARTNERS – PROCUREMENT, PRIVATISATION, PARTNERSHIPS, TRADING, AND CHOICE

Introduction

Much of the period 1979–1997 in local government was dominated by the impact of the introduction of privatisation into the delivery of local government services. The shock of this approach, in the imposition of privatisation on local government was possibly greater than the changes in working culture brought about by these processes within local government. Working with private sector and joint service delivery between local authorities had occurred before but the introduction of Compulsory Competitive Tendering (CCT) was seen as the embodiment of centralised control on local governance. Compulsion was required in part owing to the GATT/WTO international trade agreements delivered through the EU, although there was little preparation for what was to happen. Further, the implementation of local government reform in 1974 was seen to be generated by the need to create larger, more efficient units for local government delivery. The signal was in the opposite direction from what then followed. It was this lack of preparation for the continued exposure of local government services to external competition which led to the jolt to the local government system. A similar shock was felt in 1997 when the newly elected government failed to abolish competition as part of the requirements on local government despite the trailing of the notion of 'best-value' prior to the election by the Labour Party.

This chapter deals with a number of the issues which have followed as part of these competition initiatives including BV, strategic partnering, and in 2004, the 'choice agenda' which includes the voluntary community sectors as providers alongside others (HMT 2002). There has also been a consideration of wider local government procurement practices in the Byatt Review in local government (2001) and the Gershon Review of efficiency in government as a whole (HMT 2004c), which have both contributed to the generation of a discussion of more open procurement processes.

At the same time, local authorities have been allowed to commence trading again, an activity which was stopped at the time of the introduction of CCT. In powers included in the Local Government Act 2003 and followed by regulations announced in July 2004, some authorities were allowed the full use of trading powers. This is an interesting tension as pressures to source more widely will include provision from all sectors including local government. The only trading relationships which are now not fully developed in government are central to local government and vice versa. The then chairman of the Audit Commission James Strachan stated on the day after these regulations were announced that local authorities frequently delivered services better than the private sector (Strachan 2004). Local authorities are now being asked to develop a commissioning role rather than one that directly provides services (DCLG 2006a). After 25 years of promoting the role of the private sector in local government, central government has now restored an open market in which local authorities can participate as providers to any business or organisation. However, in May 1997, this seemed some way off.

Local authorities as employers

Before 1997, many local authorities identified their main role as employers rather than as service providers or community leaders. Town halls have traditionally been a major employer in any locality. Much of the concern about CCT, privatisation, and competition was about council staff. At the same time, trades unions saw privatisation as a means of undermining their position and reducing their membership. There were concerns that staff, when transferred to a new employer from local authority employment, would lose their rights for pay rates, pensions, and holiday entitlements. Protection for staff had been included within EU Directives, but there had been a delay in applying them in the United Kingdom. This was eventually rectified through the Acquired Rights Directive, the provision of Fair Employment Rights and the Transfer of Undertakings (Protection of Employment) (TUPE) Regulations 1981 (as amended) which were all included in a DETR Circular in 2001 as a supplement to the Local Government Act 1999 (DETR 2000a). This circular advised of the ways in which staff matters should be considered at each stage of a privatisation process.

More recently, there has been a greater understanding and recognition of the extent to which the quality and involvement of the labour force is an essential ingredient of a high performing council. In local authorities which have performed well in BV reviews (one of the key components of the first round of CPA scores), staff were found to have a better understanding of the councils' strategic objectives and felt more confident about proposing changes for improvement. These councils also showed better corporate leadership than others. As Sanderson et al. (2004) demonstrated, the implementation of the BV processes has contributed to creating a single organisation rather than one which is primarily departmentally or 'silo' driven. The process of the BV review was important and a major factor in demonstrating to services how they contributed to the whole. Sanderson et al. (2004) also found that where local authorities were more consistent in evaluating the effects of their services at the point of delivery this had a greater impact on performance improvement, strategic objectives, and citizen engagement. The role of front line staff is also identified as being increasingly important in the performance of authorities and the quality of their delivery (PriceWaterHouseCoopers 2004; Sanderson et al. 2004). However, many service delivery staff are not seen to have adequate time available to be involved in BV delivery improvement. Finally, it was found that involving staff in BV and other performance processes was important for staff retention (PriceWaterHouseCoopers 2004).

Privatisation

Much of the literature on privatisation of public services views the process of exposing local authority services to competition as one which is detrimental to the public service ethos, reduces service delivery standards, has a poor outcome for staff, and leads to services being driven by cost efficiencies and the 'bottom line' (Walsh 1995; Kakbadse 2003).

The process of privatisation is occurring in a more organic way with local authorities utilising privatisation for specific reasons, including cash injection to improve capital investment, or to introduce major changes to local working practices. There have been some problems in the introduction of privatised services and these generally derive from specific causes. The first is where a poor service is privatised without any other action being taken to improve it. When these failures occur, they attract much press attention and increasingly have an effect on the market rating of the private sector company which has had the contract failure. The second is where the private sector has been introduced to bring specific expertise in order to assist the management of change programme and possibly to demonstrate to inspectors and others that there is a plan to improve the situation. This approach may take some time to embed; often a weak authority may take the view that the privatisation process demonstrates commitment to seek improvement even if this has not been evidenced in practice. The third type of failure is where the local authority does not have a clear understanding of the 'client' function. All contracts need standards for performance measurement and acceptable means for dealing with contract failure. Many early privatised services had client and contract management functions which were too small for the scale of the work being outsourced and often this led to poor performance and dissatisfaction with the process.

The private sector has also learned through the process. Some contracts are difficult to manage and do not generate what is seen to be an acceptable profit margin. Although some contracts have been 'bought' as loss leaders, it is now an essential feature of contract evaluation that the purchasing authority takes into account whether the contractor is taking a reasonable view of the resources likely to be required in the delivery of the contract.

Joint service delivery between local authorities

Before local authorities were prohibited from supplying services to other councils, there was considerable experience of joint procurement and provision across a range of services including waste collection and disposal, and ITC services. These arrangements had developed through a variety of relationships over many years and were seen to be a way of reducing costs. Many local authorities had also procured these services through private contractors prior to the requirements in CCT. The introduction of CCT ended these arrangements while some local authority officers went on to establish companies such as Capita.

Many smaller arrangements for service delivery developed between local authorities, where one authority could provide a service to another based on spare capacity within an existing contract. Although the opportunities for this were limited, they were nevertheless significant in the operation of an out-of-hours emergency telephone service or specialist services such as the Public Analyst or trading standards. This approach was used widely in the implementation of the new unitary authorities from 1995 onwards. In some cases these were not long-standing agreements and were more transitional in their nature but nevertheless worked on the basis of service delivery 'at cost', that is, the costs of management and administration were included in addition to the service cost but these were not seen to be at a profit or generating a surplus.

In the late 1990s, some local authorities started to consider these approaches in a more structured way. The Welland Partnership made up of four distinct councils from three different county areas – South Kesteven from Lincolnshire, East Northamptonshire from Northamptonshire, Melton and Harborough from Leicestershire and Rutland Unitary Authority – established a new form of arrangement. The five authorities comprise a geographic area the same size as that enclosed by the M25 while they also have large areas of rural sparsity which present cost and delivery challenges to the authorities. Each district council in the Welland Partnership not only maintains its links with its traditional partners within the county but also works with its partners which have a sense of unity by being defined as a 'natural area' by English Nature (1998). The underlying geology at the edge of the Cotswold limestone and commonalty of the River Welland gives the sub-region a unity which is perceived by its residents and also presents many similar challenges. The individual district councils are also different from many of their neighbours within their counties which are in other natural areas.

In 1996, the five authorities began to discuss the potential for joint working and service delivery. This was stimulated by the introduction of BV processes and benchmarking of performance and cost data across services. The political leadership of the authorities not only included all parties, but during the period of the partnership has also changed. The sub-regional partnership has concentrated on those areas where it can work better together rather than seeking to join up all services. Initially the chief executives started to meet, which was followed by the establishment of a leaders group and finally the meeting of individual service heads. The motivation was primarily to deliver more effective and efficient services in a rural area and an early initiative was to introduce the ability to pay bill for all five authorities in any location – a move subsequently overtaken by e-government. The development of joint delivery initiatives has not always relied on all five authorities participating and the partnership work has meant that some of the five authorities are delivering on behalf of others. One early example was the provision of specialist legal advice between the five local authorities and the appointment of a legal trainee. Subsequently services such as building control and environmental health have been developed to work in a more integrated way. An early review of each authority's procurement rules and processes and the establishment of insurance indemnity cover for these arrangements created a secure platform for joint appointments and cross-border delivery. For other service provision, the Welland Partnership has sought to obtain the benefits of joint procurement for IT equipment, for example, or for the implementation of new systems. In e-government, the five authorities have taken a shared approach to leadership in the implementation of the priority outcomes for e-government (ODPM 2004e) and the use of authentication as a means of accessing services.

Strategic partnering

Although the process of BV was potentially able to bring forward all local government services to be considered for competition, the main focus has been on service performance and delivery. Competition was seen to be an important deliverable through BV but it is unclear how far this has been achieved. In some services, the private sector continued to replace locally developed approaches particularly in revenues and benefits and finance.

As a result of these less directed approaches to competition in local government, private sector suppliers began to consider the ways in which they could provide services. Strategic partnering was a new concept in which a combination of contracted service delivery could be extended to allow a Strategic Delivery Partnership to undertake additional work for other organisations or local authorities. Some of the major service suppliers envisaged the establishment of a series of regional dominant strategic partnerships where similar companies could use their business experience to develop new markets in local government by taking on their business. The nature of the contract was to be different to take advantage of local opportunities. Rather than contracting to undertake specifically defined transactions, a strategic partnership would take over a whole council's administration or the front office function.

For some local authorities, this approach looked particularly attractive as it would help to change working practices and improve efficiency as well as performance. In other cases, it would bring some guaranteed investment in IT or other facilities where councils had not been able to invest in the past. In areas where the council remained one of the principal employers, faced with a continuing wider failure in the employment market, the ability to become more efficient while attempting to expand the work available so that the council would not need to make staff redundant was seen to be an attractive proposition. For suppliers, a 10-year agreement with a local authority provided some stability and a base in the region. Competition was seen to be an expensive process for both supplier and local authorities and having a wider, longer contract would mean that further work could be included without an additional competitive process. The private sector may also have taken the view that local authorities were run very inefficiently and there would be a reasonable market in generating real cost savings.

In order to assist the development and implementation of these partnerships, the ODPM established the Strategic Partnership Taskforce (SPT) in 2001 (DETR 2001a), with the publication of a prospectus and an invitation to local authority partnerships to join in the process. The SPT was staffed by secondees from a number of major British companies interested in developing this market. Between 2001 and 2004, this team provided direct support to a wide range of emergent partnerships. The SPT also produced a series of reports and guidance for local authorities interested in pursuing these approaches, such as the Technical Notes for structures for the Public Private Partnerships (ODPM 2002a), an approach to re-thinking service delivery with provider partners (ODPM 2003j) and how to turn the general approach into an outline business case (ODPM 2003k). This approach developed by the SPT was established alongside other similar initiatives such as the Public Finance Initiative (PFI) and the work of the 4Ps established by the local government family to promote consideration of the mixed economy.

In developing some pilot support projects for emergent strategic service partnerships (SSPs), the SPT devised a definition of the characteristics of a SSP. These were that it

1 demonstrates alignment of goals between partners;
2 emphasise[s] the importance of relationships;
3 involves the delivery of services by one body on behalf of another or through joint working;
4 aspires to deliver more than a traditional contract;
5 incorporates sharing of risk and reward;
6 expects a change in behaviours between partners;
7 intends to be flexible and is able to change in scope and nature over its lifetime;
8 demonstrates trust and good communication;
9 focuses on outcomes rather than outputs;

10 demonstrates joint working (planning, monitoring, problem-solving and decision-making through a joint strategic board) and sharing of ideas and resources;
11 is based on openness and honesty (e.g. open book accounting);
12 supports continuous improvement in service delivery over its lifetime and captures corporate learning; and
13 provides mutual benefits to all partners. (ODPM 2004d, p. 8)

The work of the SPT was completed in March 2004. Its final report indicates (ODPM 2004d) that there are a number of pre-conditions which are needed to ensure that an SSP works in any authority. These include leadership and commitment together with the establishment of clear processes for decision making, while the governance arrangements were seen to be critical. The utilisation of Strategic Service Delivery Partnerships varied in practice. Some local authorities maintained a mixed portfolio of suppliers or decided to develop much smaller service agreements. In some cases, the approach to implementing an SSP was managed in a more incremental way and as Layton (2004) pointed out this was an appropriate approach to developing new authority/supplier relationships when the costs of a major partnership approach were seen to be high and the potential outcomes too risky. This incremental approach represented the development of SSP working at a more natural pace, widening as relationships grew, with more options being left until later, when the partnership had developed further. However, as Layton (2004, p. 29) also comments, there are some disadvantages in this approach as where 'the private sector hasn't got a twelve-year contract, they may not be prepared to put money up-front'.

As Strategic Service Delivery Partnerships developed alongside the emergent CPA approach in 2002, same local authorities with concerns about their potential to achieve a good score in that process turned to strategic partnering in an effort to generate some change prior to these inspections in order to demonstrate willingness and an action plan to improve performance. Some local authorities found strategic partnering and the taskforce to be useful whereas others and some suppliers found the costs associated with the protracted negotiations meant that the benefits were fewer. For some suppliers there may also have been an over-optimistic view of the potential size of the market and the savings to be made from this means of service delivery. Many local authorities had pared down operating and transactional costs as a response to the tight financial regime in the 1980s and 1990s. The suppliers did not always find that they could provide a more efficient offer. In other areas, the political issues related to the trade unions proved to be too strong to conclude an agreement. Finally the latter period of the SPT was overtaken by different policy initiatives on procurement developed for local government. The publication of the National Strategy for Public Procurement by ODPM (2003j) and the wider review of efficiency in the public sector led by Sir Peter Gershon brought different approaches. These included the requirement on each local authority to publish an annual efficiency statement and the establishment of the Regional Centres for Excellence in 2004.

The Lyons and Gershon reviews: from central to local delivery?

The review of government efficiency led by Sir Peter Gershon was launched by the Treasury in July 2004 (Gershon 2004). It was an attempt to deal with the potential uncertainties about the economy and to meet the criticism about the expansion of central government since 1997. Wider underlying pressures for a shift to 'smaller' government started in the Clinton administration in the early 1990s (Osborne and Gaebler 1992) and more recently following the work of Alesina and Spolaore (2003), which has demonstrated that smaller states are more economically successful. The size of government is now seen to be an issue which relates not only to efficient governance but also to effective governance. In Alesina's and Spolaore's work, they demonstrated that smaller, more homogenous units of government create more effective market conditions and more political stability. In Europe and within the United Kingdom, this has led to a series of long-term initiatives to support the implementation of 'new localism' (Corry et al. 2004).

In the period immediately following 1997 there was a continuation of the previous government's spending plans which were seen to be tight on public expenditure but not reductionist in their approach. This period allowed the government to determine priorities and the Treasury to develop a more corporate approach to expenditure than ever experienced before in central government. Comprehensive Spending Reviews (CSR), developed a 'star chamber' approach where ministers were made increasingly responsible for the delivery of agreed targets. The targets were included in each department's Public Service Agreement (each of which is published on the departmental web site) with funding for baseline and specific additional activities being closely associated with these expected outcomes. The process of securing implementation was followed through by the Prime Minister's Delivery Unit (PMDU). In all of these units and offices, the presence of 'outsiders', non-career civil servants started to increase from the late 1990s particularly though secondees with experience in the voluntary sector or local government, where delivery experience was seen to be greater than existed in central government.

Although the provenance of the efficiency review was clear in the move to smaller, more efficient government, commentators have also suggested that this is also in a long line of similar approaches over a number of years. Hood (2004) argues that this is a 'back to the future' initiative reminiscent of the 'unbundling' of public services in the early 1990s, where local managerial autonomy was expected to provide a more efficient use of budgets. The approach in the Spending Review announced in 2007 continues to be generated by an absolute objective to reduce the size and cost of central government. The Lyons Review (2004) on central government was an attempt to provide the means by which re-location leads to fundamental change and possible downsizing. In addition, central departments have also accepted reductions in staff numbers including the Home Office *conclusa* ~

and the Department of Health, whereas a third of the posts in DfES are expected to disappear by 2008.

One way of achieving further efficiency in government could be the movement of many services from central to local government as suggested by Lyons (2006). This would support a more integrated approach to citizen and business delivery as set out in the Varney Review (Varney 2006) while cutting down the multiple handling of cases and records by local and central government departments on the other. The reduction in the size of the civil service, particularly in London, is also seen to be part of a need to adjust to devolution. Increased powers in Scotland, Wales, and Northern Ireland leave less to do in London, although the growing debate on the need for an English Parliament may absorb some of the staff from central government.

Choice

The notion of choice in public services has largely been associated with competition processes to open up the market to a range of providers, offering to deliver a service generally in the name of the local authority. However, the notion of choice has been developing as a concept in delivery particularly in health and housing, although there is a lack of clarity in who is exercising choice – the user or the provider. Most experiments have been undertaken in the health sector where a choice of provider has been offered to those who have been on a waiting list for more than a fixed period of time. The assessment of these early pilots shows that some people prefer choice for some types of operations particularly where they are routine or urgent, although there is a need for follow-up support to make these work with confidence. There also seem to be varying definitions between public sectors, although Lent and Arend (2004, p. 12) settle for choice when 'decisions previously taken by professionals are delegated to users'. In their study, they conclude that there are policy areas where choice could be opened up but that the implications are complex and need to be considered on a case-by-case basis, that is, that there is no one way to implement increased choice. The examples which they provide relate to housing stock, community transport providers, and refuse collection. However, they are strongly of the view that the need to consider the implications on equity of the way in which choice is offered is fundamental and there is a strong necessity to ensure that the choice is really one which is open to the service user.

The growing potential for the voluntary sector

Most of the discussion about achieving cost reduction and efficiency in central and local government has been focused on privatisation. However, there has also been a growing interest in the role of the voluntary sector to deliver services. Over the past 20 years, many voluntary bodies have moved into the mixed economy, offering their services to local authorities to provide care or advice as any private sector partner, although channelling income back in to the charitable objectives of the organisation. There has also been an interest in the role of intermediaries able to help deliver public services alongside public officials.

The voluntary and community sector is changing its role. Policy developments in 2006, towards the implementation of double devolution (Miliband 2006a, 2006b), may see the role of the voluntary sector as a mechanism for local delivery in communities. The lower overheads of voluntary organisations may be counter to the price efficiencies expected from the aggregation of demand to achieve lower prices from the voluntary sector.

Conclusions

The delivery of privatised services within local authorities has continued since 1997 although without a significant degree of central government pressure, which was apparent in the immediately preceding period. The ways in which services can be delivered have widened. Although there has been little explanation of the world trade requirements for exposure of work to competition, local authority chief executives have been asked to provide details of the contracts they have let during the past year in order to fulfil the requirements of the EU returns (ODPM 2004g). After 25 years of pressure to open up work to the private sector, a new era is emerging in which a more mixed economy is likely to emerge through a greater variety of providers including the voluntary and community sector and local authorities. As yet it is unclear what kind of response will be made from the private sector in developing new forms of arrangements.

7

JOINING-UP AROUND CUSTOMERS – THE ROLE OF E-GOVERNMENT

Introduction

Since 1997, much of the government's attention has been focused on how to turn policy into action at the local level. In addition to the variety of different approaches which have been used including targetry, the CPAs, Local Public Service Agreements, and Community Strategies, there has also been an emphasis on the role of e-government to generate more immediate and personalised delivery. Initially, the use of e-government meant services delivered by the web and attracted criticism for potentially excluding those in social need who did not have access to technology. Gradually, through the development by local authorities, e-delivery has been seen to be capable of more than this means of delivery. For citizens it can mean that it is easier for them to receive assessments for services in their homes by local government officers using mobile technology, providing the familiar face-to-face service. Technology also generates considerable savings in the back office, where much of the transaction processing takes place. It can also reduce the time spent in multiple form filling for customers and repeat process-ing by the same organisation. The utilisation of an e-infrastructure also means that it is possible to offer citizens additional benefits and services that they may not be aware of, and similarly for businesses. Using back office systems such as workflow, document and records management, and Geographic Information Systems (GISs) linked to mobile and more traditional forms of working make it possible to provide a fuller assessment of need. It also makes it possible for citizens to 'self-serve' or access services by telephone or face to face in the office if they wish.

In some areas, there is low take-up by the public of the Internet to access public services although the use of digital TV or the web to follow local sports teams or book holidays suggests a greater potential use. The use of broadband has been increasing significantly each year (see eGovernment Register for individual local authority take-up figures on http://www.brent.gov.uk/crmsupplier.nsf).

The greatest barriers to the use of e-enabled approaches are the cultural ones expressed by staff and professionals. E-delivery in English local government has been associated with wide-scale BPR, an approach which reassesses and streamlines working practices. Inside local government the reorientation to customer focus is the most revolutionary outcome of e-government.

This chapter reviews these changes and also discusses the longer term potential for e-enabled local government. This may provide greater integration between services and the back office now possible with the use of technology. At a more fundamental level, these e-enabled approaches may lead to a re-making of the relationship between the state and the citizen. Since 1945 and the advent of the welfare state, services have been available but they have been supplied on the basis of application by the citizen. They have primarily been 'pull' services to the applicant, where the user has been required to request each individual service or entitlement separately rather than 'push' services from the state, where services are offered as soon as eligibility is established regardless of specific request. In the e-government era, it is possible to advise citizens of their full entitlement including services and benefits for which they had no knowledge and for which they may not have pursued a claim. These new approaches can provide additional services and resources to the most needy, who are unaware of their entitlements. It is also possible to target specific groups for benefit or support in new ways.

The problems of silo government for the citizen

Government initiatives are characterised as individual, with people being treated separately by each service which they encounter. Although these initiatives are frequently targeted at specific population groups or localities, this approach also risks missing need. There is also evidence that initiatives are working against each other. This has been a concern across the world since the early 1990s that resulted in a major switch in policy emphasis to JUG. This re-focusing has occurred in Canada, New Zealand, and Australia, for example. As Perri 6 et al. (1999) describe it,

> The aim was to move away from organising budgets, targets, incentives, management structures and accountability around the administration of functions, towards achieving outcomes and finding solutions. (p. 16)

The ability to focus on the customer rather than the provider has now become a constant theme in public policy. This move to JUG has also been emphasised by the growing number of cases where people or communities have been failed through separate working practices of different agencies and the confusion about the means and legalities of sharing information. These cases range from working with children – as in the Climbie case and the Soham murders – to the case of an elderly couple dying after their gas supply had been cut off (December 2003).

In all incidences the ability of organisations to share information and common working practices would have assisted the victims. There are also concerns for citizens who may need to report information several times over or have to provide slightly different information to agencies. The most frequent outcome of this is the failure of the state to see citizens and places as a whole.

In addition to the benefits of JUG to the citizen there are also savings in the administrative support for service delivery, in re-entering or 'double keying' data into records, keeping records up to date and also managing information relationships with other agencies. Perri 6 et al. (1999) summarise these benefits as listed earlier in Chapter 2, p. 20.

There are also other concerns about the extent to which citizens and localities can engage in debates with public agencies about priorities. Large public bodies are seen to be impenetrable. Overall, there is an assumption that a 'healthy' democracy is one in which 'there are major opportunities for the mass of ordinary people actively to participate' (Crouch 2000, p. 1). Some of those who enter this debate are concerned with the theory of the modern state. Much of this debate relies on improving models of engagement between citizens and government, whether central or local, based on a traditional relationship which primarily revolves around the professional or official's view of what is best for the citizen. This is now more widely seen as the producer's view. These traditional relationships are based on professional definitions of services within prescribed rules. The failure to join services around citizens and increase democratic engagement has supported the implementation of local e-government. The prime minister established a target of 100% e-enablement of public services for December 2005 in his *Modernising Government White Paper* (Cabinet Office 1999).

The use of technology has also proved to be effective for those who have mobilised around causes. There has been a surge in these activities since 2000 and include the countryside marches, the fuel demonstrations (Doherty et al. 2003) and local cause groups, which have been able to defeat sitting MPs in pursuance of local issues.

Implementing local e-government

The opportunities presented by e-government may be considerable. Local accountability is now seen to be closer to delivery. The pre-conditions for change are related to the objective of devolved responsibility (OPSR 2002) and the significant growth in confidence in the ability of local government to perform well as demonstrated by the CPA process (Audit Commission 2002e). However, these changed conditions go further. The delivery of e-government at the local level is joined up and citizen focused in its outcome objectives. It was set seven critical tests of success:

1 joined up in ways that make sense to the customer
2 accessible

3   delivered (or supported) electronically
4   delivered jointly
5   delivered seamlessly
6   open and accountable
7   used by citizens. (e-gov@local DETR 2002)

The leadership for delivery at the local level was political, through the appointment of an e-champion, and the success of delivery was monitored through a BV performance indicator BVPI 157 which required demonstration of 100% of local e-enablement across 10 generic transactions by December 2005, and which was almost fully achieved by 2006. Additionally, local authorities were invited to work in partnership with other councils for joint delivery to citizens, and development of citizen-focused products for e-enabled delivery were developed by local authorities for each other. These latter approaches, largely encompassed in a programme of national projects, included central government departments to develop locally joined-up processes.

Another factor which may have some bearing on this differing approach to delivery is that the policy and implementation of the programme was generated by former senior local government officers working in central government (Morphet 2003a) forming the Local Government Modernisation Team (LGM). These approaches offered new meaning to JUG and its application in reform of citizen delivery. E-government is also seen to be a critical component in delivering efficiencies through the Gershon Review which required all local authorities to achieve 2.5% savings each year from 2005 which are to be taken from the back office and put into investment in front line services. By 2006, local authorities had already exceeded this target.

In building capacity to deliver e-government, the LGM team learned from some of the delivery models used by the other government departments for local government, particularly the requirements for targeted funding to achieve specific performance outcomes. In order to support this at the local level, councils were invited to prepare their own action plans to achieve e-government, known as Implementing Electronic Government (IEG) statements (ODPM 2003o, 2004k). Although some common content was requested, councils were able to show how they were to reach the e-government target by using locally set programmes and initiatives. The approach adopted was not prescriptive on the order of the actions or the way in which the e-government programme was to be implemented. This allowed each council to use its IEG statement to support local objectives and to work within its own legacy contracts. This approach was much criticised by suppliers and some other parts of government. However, the LGM team sought a willing acceptance of the target from local government.

In return for preparing a satisfactory IEG statement, a funding allocation to each individual local authority was offered from the £660m. funds on a flat-rate basis. This was also innovative. The LGM team recognised that to have a joined-up approach to local government e-government meant that district councils would need a disproportionate amount of help. These smaller councils had not had the cash injections provided by the DoH and DfES in earlier years. They also have a much higher level of citizen transactions, and hence would need proportionately greater funding. It was also assumed that larger councils could generate more efficiencies from improving processes.

At this early stage, councils were encouraged to work together to ensure that they obtained the benefits of joint procurement or shared expertise. Further, a partnership fund for joined-up approaches across local authorities, which was eventually released in July 2002, was trailled. Councils had the opportunity to develop capacity building. The programme had some early successes. The Audit Commission (2002c) report *Message Beyond the Medium* demonstrated that within a year of IEGs being submitted for the first time, over 90% of councils were working together.

Many councils considered the e-government agenda to be costly and risky in technological terms. The LGM team proposed a series of early projects that would provide real-life models and even software or systems for councils to use. In encouraging low-cost innovative solutions developed directly by councils, the team was seeking to encourage acceptable, local government owned solutions that would work. Given the success of the approach to these early projects, a series of national projects covering both developing e-government infrastructure and service links was defined. In the service projects the links were not only between local authorities but also with central government services.

Local implementation of e-government

In comparison with central government, local authorities deliver a greater range of services to people in a wider range of personal situations. Some popular estimates suggest that over 80% of all public services are delivered by local authorities. These range from purchasing a garden recycling bag to serious child protection issues. As a consequence of this, local authorities decided that single-channel access is not an option. Rather, local authorities offer a range of channels so that citizens can use their channel of choice for any particular service (DTLR 2001a). Until 2005 there was a focus on web-only delivery in central government although this was widened to include public interface through contact centres (phone and face to face) following the publication of the Transformational Government Strategy (Cabinet Office 2005).

However, local authorities also quickly saw that e-enablement could help to streamline the back office to provide more joined-up citizen services. Although there is an efficiency driver in this approach, it is primarily focused on resolution of all issues at the first contact and using multi-service contact centres. Some local authorities are already resolving over 80% of service requests at the first point of contact with the council. This is engineering a fundamental change in the philosophy of public service delivery in England – that the council takes the responsibility for drawing together all entitlements and services for citizens based on eligibility rather than citizens having to explore the system or to use intermediaries to help them. This develops the notion of the individual citizen or business account – a concept that is growing into delivery. Once implemented, it will put local authorities into the same position as major private sector service businesses where it is possible to manage relationships through a single point, whether it is web, phone, or face to face. Being able to recognise a returning customer is a key element of the web-based business model and is used to extend the relationship between the customer and the provider, such as the approach used by Amazon.co.uk. In this approach, Amazon suggests to customers other choices which other customers have selected: 'Those who bought this, also enjoyed/bought that'. This notion of identifying interest and developing a lasting relationship is new but developing within local government.

The immediate contact with citizens, regardless of the channel, is increasingly likely to be supported by the use of a customer relations management (CRM) system, which can track customers or citizens through these different points of contact. A CRM can ensure that the organisation knows that it is dealing with the same person. Personal needs can be profiled to ensure that people receive the best service. This process can be extended so that a call or e-mail, which is automatically put into the back office system, can be performance managed, and commitment accounted. The process can be transparent throughout its passage through the system by the citizen on the web site, at home, in the library, or through digital TV. The same information can be used by staff engaged in face-to-face processes or on the phone, using the same technology.

Local authorities were required to demonstrate their e-enablement progress through the delivery of 10 generic transactions that cover every aspect of the council's business:

1 Providing information
2 Collecting revenue
3 Providing benefits and grants
4 Consultation
5 Regulation
6 Application for services
7 Booking venues, courses and resources
8 Paying for goods and services
9 Providing access to community, professional or business networks
10 Procurement. (DETR 2000a)

In order to deliver in ways that are joined up to the citizen, local authorities also took the view that they could go further. Not only would it be helpful if all services within the local authority could be delivered jointly but also these should be joined in some way to those public services which are delivered by other organisations. For planning matters, this was seen to provide far greater integration with other agencies such as the Environment Agency, Fire Service, Health and Safety Executive (www.parsol.gov.uk). This could also be extended across neighbouring areas to reduce the impact of administrative and geographical boundaries where this made sense to the user. In planning, there are obvious benefits and user synergies in joined-up regulation and enforcement processes where often a number of organisations are involved at different points in the process. This also extends to consultees on planning policy and applications.

There are also considerable efforts being made to deliver local authority services across local authority administrative boundaries. Some of this partnership working is developing rapidly in areas of two-tier government, where interlocking services can be delivered at differing tiers. The ability of the upper tier to offer lower tier services and vice versa is now being developed using the same portals and CRM systems. However, there is no evidence that local democratic accountability at the local level is being lost with authority branding and accountability being maintained. Partnerships are developing joint service delivery in addition to the 'no boundaries approach to service access'. The Welland Partnership in the East Midlands is possibly one of the most developed sub- regional partnership in England in this respect where it is possible to transact business for any authority across the partnership. Other joined-up service delivery methods are being developed by working with other public agencies, for example, with the police in East Riding, health in Herefordshire, and fire in Devon. In other localities, the development of more comprehensive joined-up approaches across members of the LSP are leading to joint delivery to citizens with specific initiative being developed in Hartlepool, Herefordshire, and Harrow. Other councils are seeking to join up delivery outlets to ensure that the first-time resolution concept is being extended. Some are achieving this through an assets review of all property owned by the LSP, as in, Stockport and in Somerset Care Direct pilots schemes are joining up social care and benefit payments, or in Wychavon and Suffolk where joined up public services are being offered across multiple governance levels.

In addition to the prime minister's target for e-government achievement in local and central government, the EU has also identified e-government as one of the major fields of activity in e-Europe (CEC 2003). In this programme, which was formally adopted on 21 February 2003, the action plan has identified a common list of basic public services, which lists 20 transactions that the member state governments have agreed upon to be benchmarked across the EU. This list of services includes applications for building permission which is assumed to be planning consent. The other transactions deal with issues such as change of address, car registration and enrolment in higher education. Achievement of these targets is to be benchmarked (CEC 2002) and includes not only the number of services available on the web but also the use of the web in defined monitored transactions – obtaining information, obtaining forms and returning completed forms. There is also a supplementary indicator that each member state is asked to identify – how many public transactions are integrated with the back office.

Developing and implementing priority outcomes

Much of the effort in the latter stages of the local e-government programme was directed towards achieving the take up of e-enabled services, achieving efficiency reform and moving further on the 'personalisation' agenda. All of these additional approaches have supported the roll out and take up of e-government services.

During 2004, the ODPM issued a list of 'Priority Outcomes' which it proposed all local authorities should pursue. This list was a subset of the 10 generic transactions and was seen as a means of providing citizens and businesses with some common expectations of local authority e-enabled services.

Priority outcomes for local e-government

1 school admissions
2 community information
3 democratic renewal
4 local environment
5 e-procurement
6 payments
7 libraries, sport and leisure
8 transport
9 benefits
10 support for vulnerable people
11 supporting new ways of working
12 accessibility of services
13 high take up of web transaction services making it easier for citizens to do business with the council. (ODPM 2004e)

These priority outcomes did much to focus the effort of local authorities in delivering e-enabled services in England. The subsequent campaigns to improve take-up of e-services in 2006 together with the pressures to achieve efficiencies have all supported the further development of e-services.

The barriers to citizen engagement and delivery

The contract between the citizen and the state, whether in the existing or new form, is likely to depend, from the citizen's perspective, on the ways in which these interactions work. This will include how easy they are to access and the credibility of the outcome. The key elements are:

1 *Form of interaction* – is it easy to use?
2 *Initiatives to be considered* – how meaningful are they?
3 *Decisions* – are they at least in part dependent on the interaction?
4 *Organisational cultures* – are these amenable to the interaction and its potential outcome?
5 *Administrative silos* – are these preventing access? Do organisations treat me as the same person without multiple provision of the same information?
6 *Professionalism* – are boundaries preventing joined-up delivery?
7 *Tracking* – can I always find out where my requests are in the process?
8 *Citizens or subjects* – am I central to the process or am I lucky to get what is given?

Concerns have regularly been expressed about low levels of take up of web-based services – people prefer to use the phone (Portfolio Communications 2003). Those in greatest need of government services, such as the poor or the elderly, do not have access to the Internet. However, experience in the delivery of e-government services in Portugal, for example, shows that village mediators can have an important impact on delivery improvement in rural areas (Moreira 2003). Also, the adoption of multi-channel access to public services in local and now central government should help to address these potential criticisms. Citizens should be able to access their services through channels of their choice.

E-government provides local tools of governance and delivery, which can begin to overcome these barriers although they need to be combined with organisational and political will. Easier transactions do not improve the experience if they remain separate or low in relevance. The combination of channels can improve the *means* as citizens can use the method they prefer on each occasion. At the same time, the citizen should be able to obtain added value from each transaction regardless of the means, so that requests for one service can lead to the offer of others which could be available or relevant. Although e-government cannot make any difference to the issues that are available for JUG or a more participative style, it can start to provide comparisons between practices at the local level with the potential for creating new acceptable norms of activity.

The provision of e-government also creates more transparency (Flinders 2002) with less ability to withhold information. Issues that have also been primarily regarded as *professional* can also be opened to wider participation through e-government. This can occur in a variety of ways – through greater provision of information about entitlement rules, viewing progress of applications and cases and also though the development of one-stop delivery for services, which can expose specific services to more detached performance monitoring. E-government can also provide more information not only on the issue but also during the process of decision making (Murray and Greer 2002).

E-government cannot remove all the barriers to joint working between professionals, but the ability to join case records or track those in the system changes the parameters of potential delivery. One recent example of this is a new information-sharing approach for children potentially at risk because different parts of the public protection system are not joined up. This is being implemented through the Children Act 2004. Another is in the joint provision for adult support being developed through Care Direct. These joined-up systems encourage an open debate between professional groups on differing service protocols. They also allow for all appropriate staff to be able to access and contribute to records, enabling case-tracking regardless of child or adult movements and multiple agency involvement.

E-government cannot change the nature of the content of *decisions* and this remains a matter for political determination. However, it can assist in changing the climate of what can be considered and how this can be done. The same is true of organisational cultures although the openness of e-government can create a context within which internally driven producer cultures are less acceptable. Where JUG is needed around the citizen, existing cultures can be challenged particularly when these services are e-enabled. Reforms including BPR may assist in removing long-established working practices where these persist. The same is true of administrative silos where these are preventing access to service and entitlement. Organisations can now treat citizens as the same person without multiple provision of the same information. Services can be offered proactively rather than the weight of responsibility for service access being primarily on the citizen. Citizens can track the progress of their own business and organisations will be more exposed to dealing with the causes of delay. Poor access to service will no longer be used as a means of rationing service delivery.

Finally, e-government can encourage the development of active citizenship. Entitlement can be clearer and more accessible and related to individual circumstances. Public agencies can start to provide added value. The reduced distance between the service and the responsible organisation can help improve accountably. Increased expectations of citizen-centred delivery methods, which are transparent, participative, and clearly monitored can all serve to change this state/citizen contract. Citizens can be central to the process rather than feel lucky with what they are given.

Efficiency and e-government

One of the longer term objectives of the local e-government programme was to encourage local authorities to work more efficiently. As the Gershon efficiency agenda developed in local government then specific initiatives were measured to demonstrate both cash and cashless savings arising from e-government investment. This investment has come in a variety of forms including strategic partnerships for shared service delivery (e.g. Liverpool, Suffolk, and Rotherham with BT), or other forms of working such as the implementation of e-procurement. Each local authority was asked to submit an Annual Efficiency Statement. The efficiency lead from local government, Barry Quirk, suggested that efficiency could come from doing

- More for less
- Much more for a little more
- Less for more
- The same for less. (Quirk/ODPM 2005)

By December 2006, local authorities were reported as being on course to meet their Gershon efficiency targets one year early (OGC 2006).

Conclusions: changing the citizen's relationship with government?

The use of e-government is part of a broader trend in society where service has become more individual and is tailored to the specific requirements of the customer (Illsley et al. 1999; Audit Commission 2003). These pressures and the governmental challenges are increasingly demanding different responses from current government service providers. There are pressures for all services to join a more mainstream delivery to citizens (Illsley et al. 1999; Ling 2002). As yet very little has been written about this issue other than generic studies of the use of Internet for transactions. Although there are those who have considerable concerns about the use of e-government technology for all groups (Graham 2002), there are others (Grieco 2000) who demonstrate how 'wired' government re-introduces local and community decision making. There is evidence that age and class groups are less likely to use web or text messaging as a means of undertaking transactions services but for other age groups this is the almost exclusive means of communication.

These changes change the citizen and state contract. E-government has the potential to make a considerable direct contribution to more localised processes whilst indirectly changing expectations of how citizens are engaged with government and governance. The changes being generated within government service providers are moving the citizen's expectation that it is the government that will be proactive in provision. In this case, the state will

- be responsible for joining up policy and delivery
- tailor services to individual needs
- provide added value at the point of contact

and the citizen will choose the channel or means of delivery.

These changes are already in progress and are due to become widely available in every local authority. They could provide entirely new models of governance, which will require a new balance in the state–citizen relationship. These changes were planned and are foretold in *Modernising Government* in 1999 (Cabinet Office).

8

COUNCILLORS, STANDARDS, AND CORRUPTION

Introduction

There have always been concerns about councillor conduct in local government. The temptations have been significant. Pressure created to award contracts to local businesses or to friends have always been present and represented in novels such as *This Sporting Life* by David Storey, *Life at the Top* by John Braine, and in the poetry of John Betjeman. The late 1990s were also dogged by a series of high-profile council corruption cases in Doncaster and Rotherham, where councillors were prosecuted for various acts of misconduct including accepting bribes for planning consents and for misusing council funds. Similar scandals have also hit some Welsh local authorities and agencies.

The attempt to 'clean up' local government was seen to be a key feature of the post-1997 regime, with the 1998 White Paper indicating that each local authority in England would need to adopt a Councillor Code of Conduct and a Standards Board. This was accompanied by the establishment of the Standards Board for England to which any citizen could address a complaint about a councillor. Until this time, the chief executive, an employee of the council, had to discipline individual councillors without any direct sanctions other than those offered by the offending member's political party group. This was seen as a weak system, not least as it depended on self-management while chief executives could be vulnerable in their own posts if their attempts to hold investigative hearings were unwelcome. The role of external auditors had also been seen to be significant before 1997, with some high-profile cases being pursued such as the 'Homes for Votes' case at Westminster City Council against its former leader Dame Shirley Porter. Here there were accusations that specific council properties were privatised in order to shift the local electoral profile and thus influence the local elections.

The relationship between officers and elected councillors has also been seen as an important one with councillors sometimes being accused of bullying officers. These have been some of the most frequent sources of internal complaints.

Any obvious indication that a complaint or concern was about fraud is passed directly to the police for investigation. Another source of concern has arisen following cases involving children, and many local authority chief executives have subjected councillors, with official council roles related to children, to reviews by the Criminal Record Bureau. A number of councillors have also been found using council PCs, which they have in their own home, to visit 'banned' web sites and this has led to an increase in member disciplinary action in this area.

Finally, there have been concerns about the loss of a general public service ethos in the face of increased privatisation. This is seen to have an influence on the culture of local government as a whole and to change the way in which it views its primary role. In the past, many councillors regarded the local authority's role as primarily that of an employer, and local authorities have traditionally been the largest employers in their areas. This has meant, in some cases, that councillors have been unwilling to promote change or to support management and disciplinary actions against officers who have been found to be contravening employment rules.

The system before the Local Government Act 2000

Before 2000, there was a National Code of Conduct for elected members, which was adopted in 1974. This was extended after the publication of the Widdicombe Committee Report on the Conduct of Local Authority Business in 1986, when specific recommendations about councillor conduct were included in the 1989 Local Government and Housing Act. Widdicombe's recommendations included

1   opening up all local authority documents to public access;
2   opening up committees to opposition parties;
3   the ending of co-option;
4   the bar on senior officers of one council being a councillor of another local authority;
5   the requirement that local authority chief executives could only be dismissed by a majority of two-thirds of the council;
6   restrictions on special advisors;
7   limits on the attendance of officers at political meetings;
8   procedures to appoint officers on merit;
9   increased powers for the Audit Commission and the local authority ombudsman;
10 a proposed review of the relationship between local authorities, enterprise boards, and regeneration.

The 1989 Act implemented some of these recommendations, and included others which were seen to be more stringent than the Widdicombe Committee's recommendations. Those included within the act were

1   the requirement of the council to establish a post of monitoring officer;
2   the requirement to establish the post as head of the paid service;

3   the 1988 Finance Act which gave finance officers the ability to report if the council was likely to act in a way which was illegal;
4   the creation of the post of returning officer for the conduct of elections;
5   powers limiting the expenditure on economic development; and
6   the limitation of the role of local authorities within companies.

Each councillor was subject to the code. This covered their ability to work in the public sector to take part in any decision making in which they had a personal or financial interest. These interests have to be declared after election and placed on an open register, and are required to include the financial interest of partners, family members, or businesses if these were likely to be material to decision making at the council. These can also be party political relationships.

In addition to the new processes applying to councillors and their behaviour, complaints against specific council decisions could be taken to the local authority ombudsman who could decide to investigate any decision to see whether maladministration had occurred. The ombudsman has powers to investigate and to recommend courses of action including the payments of damages.

The Nolan Committee on Standards in Public Life

The code of conduct for elected councillors came into force in 1989, but there remained concerns about the general conduct of local government business and the public's perception of its 'fairness'. The Nolan Committee was set up to consider 'Standards in Public Life' which looked at local government as well as other bodies. The Nolan Committee reported on local government in 1998 with proposals to change the National Code of Conduct of Local Government to that where every council had its own standards board and had adopted a code of conduct which was based on a new model code. These proposals were contained in the Third Report of the Committee on Standards in Public Life on Standards of Conduct in Local Government. Each local authority code was required to contain some general principles:

- Community leadership
- Duty to uphold the law
- Constituencies
- Selflessness
- Integrity and propriety
- Hospitality
- Decisions
- Objectivity in decision making
- Accountability
- Openness
- Confidentiality
- Stewardship

- Participation
- Declaration
- Relations with officers. (DETR 1998, figure 5)

These principles were included in the Local Government Act 2000 together with a Code of Conduct and the provision of a Local Standards Board. Reviewing progress in the implementation of the act at the local level, Stoker et al. (2003) found that 85% of councils had adopted the model code with others adding to the model code of conduct in some way. Only two councils had adopted it by default. The size of standards committees varied but Stoker et al. (2003) found that 50% were chaired by an independent person while the appointment of independent persons was seen to be generally unproblematic. However, this research did find that in some cases the standards boards took a passive role towards their work rather than a proactive one, seemingly not regarding it as an important activity. The importance of training for all councillors in conduct issues particularly in relation to planning was generally adopted as good practice.

The Standards Board for England

The principles for councillor conduct were put in effect when the Standards Board for England was established in 2001 (www.standardsboard.co.uk). The Standards Board takes complaints from any individual without evidence being required. Local authority chief executives also refer complaints about councillors which they receive to the board. In 2003–2004, the board received 3,566 complaints. The type of complaints varied:

- prejudicial interest 22%
- bringing local authority into disrepute 20%
- failure to disclose personal interest 17%
- failing to treat others with respect 12%
- using position to confer or secure advantage or disadvantage 12%
- failure to register financial interests 3%
- other 14%. (Cumulative complaints from April 2004, the Standards Board for England)

Planning

Given the temptations at the local level, and the high value which planning consent can bring to a land owner and a developer, the Nolan Committee has reported specifically on these issues. This was also seen to be an area of general public distrust of council activity. The Nolan Committee (1998) recommended that councillors who sit on planning committees should be specifically trained. The reforms went further in the Local Government Act 2000, where the planning and licensing functions were required to be taken separately from other planning

decisions and also to be taken by a committee constituting of members who w̶
not part of the executive. This was intended to generate a separation betv̶
councillors promoting schemes for regeneration or asset management and t̶
councillors involved in assessing them, separately those councillors
determine planning applications from those implementing them.

By 2006, there were moves to reverse this position. Planning was seen to be too
detached from the executive inside the local authority. Following the proposals to
integrate planning with the strategic plans and programmes for the local area in
the Sustainable Community Strategy, this separation has been challenged (DCLG
2006).

The conduct of local authority staff

The conduct of local authority staff has always been a less complex matter as it is
covered by employment law and Nolan did not recommend taking any further
action other than the addition of the Whistleblowers' Charter.

Local relationships may bring pressure to bear on key officers, particularly in
relation to report concerns about councillor behaviour. The 'protection' given to
statutory officers, that is, the chief executive, the monitoring officer, and the chief
finance officer has been strengthened. Although provisions against dismissal of the
chief executive (or the head of paid service) had existed since the 1989 Act, these
were extended to the other two statutory officers in the Local Government Act
2000. Since then, there has been considerable pressure from the Local Authorities
Employer's Association to reduce the protection given to these officers, with successive rounds of proposals. The Employer's Association argument relates primarily
to situations where trust is held to have broken down between the officers and
members. There have also been some high-profile cases where local authority
chief executives have had serious disagreements with their councillors. In these
cases it is usually the officer who leaves the local authority.

There has been much debate about the role of officers in relation to elected
councillors. There has been criticism of professionalism creating a strong set of
cultures which stand against elected councillors. This is frequently termed as
being a 'producer culture' which implies that the interests of the staff are being set
above the democratic decision-making process as well as the people who are being
served. There is certainly no doubt that the role of officer culture and the willingness to work for the public and deliver the political will are important features in
local government. As Pratchett and Wingfield (1996) state,

Often better paid, better qualified, better informed (through professional networks and
so on) and more experienced than their political counterparts, it is difficult to deny that
local government officers make a significant contribution to the overall policy process in
local authorities and to the more general nature of democracy at the local level. (Pratchett
and Wingfield 1996, p. 106)

Public service ethics

In the post-1979 period, with the introduction of competition and competitive tendering in local government it has been argued that this is undermining the public service ethos and fundamentally changing the way in which public services are managed and delivered. This has also been a concern expressed by some trades unions and local government think tanks. Some studies have examined these claims in more detail. Pratchett and Wingfield (1996, p. 107) undertook a study on whether 'the changes of the last fifteen years are subverting and undermining the public service ethos that has characterised public organisations throughout the twentieth century'. In a survey conducted in four different local authorities they sought to examine the extent to which the officers in these authorities had a public service ethos. The survey looked at five dimensions of this concept including accountability, bureaucratic behaviour, sense of community, motivation, and loyalty. Over 77% of the respondents indicating that they believed a public service ethos existed. The study found some movement away from a more bureaucratic behaviour to one which is more innovative, but concluded that division into business units internally was leading to less of a community of interest. The authors place the blame for these changes in both the competition requirements introduced into local government and the 'new public management'. However, not all the changes which were found were seen to be negative or a reduction in the public ethos as in some areas they were evolving in new ways of demonstrating accountability and the overt measurement in quality and efficiency were noted.

There have also been other concerns about the loss of a 'public service ethos'. One concern is the pressure to perform and the role of the private sector in delivery might suggest that public service ethic has been undermined. This may be the view of staff delivering services and from local authority councillors who have the democratic mandate and accountability. There have also been concerns of 'over-politicisation' of officials – local government officers who in some way lose their 'impartiality'. These officers may be appointed because they are in sympathy with the political aims of the organisation and explicitly be working to these ends rather than being impartial.

Some chief executives argue that there needs to be synergy and sympathy between the chief executive and the leading councillors for the authority to progress, although others may dispute the extent to which this is required. Some chief executives have been elected councillors earlier on in their careers, including some long-serving chief executives in London boroughs. Many local authorities require their chief executives to live within the local authority area as a job condition while there are those who consider that this creates a loss of distance in the respective roles of councillors and officers. However, it has been found in CPA inspections that good and respected working relationships between councillors and officers are fundamental to excellent local authorities.

Conclusions

The conduct of local authority councillors has been the subject of considerable debate in the period since 1986. The Widdicombe Committee recommendations were seen to be draconian and it may be doubtful whether they would survive challenges under the Human Rights Act some 20 years later. What is interesting is that the position of elected councillors is now be almost the reverse of that imposed by the government following the Widdicombe Review. Elected mayors and senior councillors on the executive can have sizeable allowances which are, in effect, salaries but provided by the local authority to which they are elected rather than another one with whom they were employed. There is some discussion about removing the political restrictions from officers. This may presage a greater combining of these roles.

One of the greatest concerns is the extent to which public service ethics can be supported through codification and legislation. There may also need to be greater protection for whistleblowers with codes of trust and the removal of fear of reprisals. In this case, whistleblowers may only be those who consider that they have little to lose in their employment circumstances, whereas those who have a lifetime invested in a single employer may take the view that this is an action that is too risky.

There may also be differences in organisations with different recruitment cultures. In local government, where there is a culture of moving between local authorities, the accessibility of other job opportunities may mean that people will move to another local authority rather than blow the whistle. In other organisations, such as civil service, there is an assumption of life-long career management which means that staff have to gain promotion from within and staff may therefore be less willing to whistle blow or even raise issues.

The extent to which ethical dilemmas placed on members and officers differ now from 20 years ago is one of conjecture. At a time when the ethical code was less well utilised in public life, these issues may not have had a strong role. Circumstantial evidence from fiction of the 1950s and the 1960s suggests an understanding that certain behaviours were inappropriate in public life whilst there was also some recognition that some of those attracted to public life were motivated by reasons of potential personal advancement.

There has also been an assumption made by those commenting on the utilisation of the New Public Management Model that behaviours of politicians and officials have in some way been 'compromised' or shifted in a culture which is now more dominated by a private sector focus. In particular, 'the meaning of some traditional public service values have been altered – such as a greater focus on results than process' (Kakabadse et al. 2003, p. 479). However, the publication of the CPA results for local authorities in 2004 showed that local government now more frequently outperforms the private sector (*Guardian*, 8 December 2004).

Local authorities are equivalent in size to big businesses and their accountability for the use of public funds places their officers and councillors under more scrutiny than the private sector. However, of all the complaints made to the Standards Board for England, some 55% are not referred for further investigation, and of those referred, 52% demonstrated no breach or no sanction to be applied and over half of these complaints are now dealt with locally (Standards Board Annual Review 2006–2007). Local government is always open to those who wish to perpetrate fraud but its dealings are more transparent and open to investigation than ever before and has been supported by the implementation of the Freedom of Information Act 2005. Public trust is only as good as the last criminal conviction. In 2004, the former leader of Lincolnshire County Council was sent to prison for using his position to influence planning proposals for his own gain. This demonstrates that the new approach since 2000 has teeth and may serve to improve public confidence as it was intended.

9

THE FUTURE OF LOCAL GOVERNMENT FINANCE

Introduction

budget

Finance is at the heart of any fundamental debate about the role of local government in the United Kingdom. It has two key dimensions – the relationship between local government and the state and the relationship between local government and the citizen. In the period of the creation of *Modern Local Government* since 1997, every reform has been directed at these two key relationships without changing the fundamental financial framework. Local authorities have been offered more freedoms and flexibilities through the Local Government Act 2000 and the reduction in requirements for councils defined as 'excellent' in CPA processes. Local authorities have been required to change their democratic structures and embody them in local written constitutions to provide more transparent decision making and a greater resource at the local level has been formed by the 'back bench members'. Local authorities have been enjoined to experiment with different methods of voting, new forms of citizen engagement and feedback, focus groups, scrutiny, and neighbourhood working.

Yet, none of these reforms has dealt with the fundamental issue of finance. It is hard for local authorities to be independent bodies, despite having contracts with government for delivery, when they are so highly dependent on central government funding. Second, while this situation prevails, the local elections continue to produce either an apathetic response or a judgement on the party in power in central government – both being indications of the perceived restricted ability of local politicians to influence major policy and expenditure decisions. Local government finance has become a trope for central–local relations and its solution is seen as the means of changing the relationship from agency to one between equals.

Some of the initiatives implemented since 1997 have started to address these issues. For example, the implementation of CPA processes followed by the league tables devised to illustrate relative performance have begun to show that while funding is important it is also the way in which resources are used at the local level that can create the added value – leadership, culture, management, and benchmarking can all make a significant difference. There has also been a recognition of some of the challenges created by complex funding streams, such as the fragmented pots of funding directed through ABIs and the 'tied' or 'passported' funding arrangements used by some central government departments to fetter any local discretion. There has also been recognition that central government requirements on local government each year are not met by associated funding increases. Several measures are in place to improve this position, from a fundamental review of local government funding, to an increase of 'freed up' money through internal efficiency savings, increased revenues through fees, charges and fines, and other specific schemes such as those for business growth. This chapter reviews this increasingly subtle picture of change, which may have significant and incremental effects on the relationships between the state and local government which in turn may change the local democratic relationship with the citizen.

Local government's constitutional role and finance

From 1888 to 2000, local government was not able to act or spend without specific legal powers, which were contained in many different pieces of legislation. The powers were not streamlined and it was frequently possible to find local authorities using different powers to undertake similar activities. Although the powers allowed the majority of authorities to do most things, the nature of the relationship was one of complex control of local government by central government. This was compounded by the development of the role of local government as a delivery agency for central government programmes in the immediate post-war period (Morphet 1993a), a tendency which was strongly emphasised by Conservative governments between 1979 and 1997. Mrs Thatcher's animosity towards local government and its competence generated an increased climate of distrust and control. This relationship started to improve slightly in the early 1990s, when Michael Heseltine became Secretary of State for the Environment, but the change in government in 1997 brought with it considerable expectations about freedom and reform. These expected reforms focused on the provision of a 'general power of competence' for local authorities, which would mean a defined role for local government within the state. The implication of this is that specific legal powers are not required to support every specific action in each local authority. The United Kingdom is one of the few countries in the EU not to have this constitutional position for local government. The implication of such a power would be that local authorities would both be free to act and also to raise revenue in ways seen in other countries such as local income tax, sales taxes, tourist taxes, or other specific charges.

The response from government did not go so far. The Local Government Act 2000 created the duty on local authorities to promote 'economic, social, and environmental well-being' which also allowed them to utilise resources for these ends without any further specific legal powers. It therefore became a power of first resort to be used before others and is seen to be fundamental and strong in its capacity to support action. This duty cannot overcome specific restrictions in legislation (which exist for any organisation) and the provisions of the Local Government Act 2000 specifically excluded finance powers for raising taxation, trading, and fees and charges, although action was promised on each of these issues subsequently. The Local Government Act 2003 conferred powers on local authorities to trade, while new specific means of raising revenue have been generated in some places such as congestion charging in London, which the mayor has hypothecated to expenditure on transport.

Central direction and local discretion – assessing the boundaries

Although much of the local government case for their control of local resources can be upheld, there has also been an issue of the quality or value for money (VFM) achieved for all local expenditure since 1997. Before this, the Audit Commission, established in 1992, had taken a strong VFM approach to local government which it progressed through a series of specific service-based studies. It reviewed issues such as property, how elected members were spending their time, and planning processes. In reviewing an individual service, the Audit Commission started to demonstrate, through the use of evidence, that local authorities could have very different degrees of effectiveness in delivery of services and outcomes with the same pattern of resources. The introduction of BV in 1997 operationalised this approach across all local authority services, encouraged the introduction and use of benchmarking within and between services, and started to look at more fundamental issues such as the effects of leadership, performance management systems, and BPR. The Audit Commission approach was fundamental to taking a wider view of auditing and assessment. Instead of merely looking at the cheapest cost, the reviews looked at VFM achievement against a wider set of targets including effectiveness for its client community. This performance-based approach developed into CPA in 2003 and will move further when CAA (DCLG 2006) is implemented in 2009.

A performance-based approach has both supported and undermined the funding debate with central government. Local authorities have been pressurised to use their funding more effectively through the setting of targets, assessment, peer review, and benchmarking. This approach has now moved to a second phase where local authorities are being pressed to improve their own efficiency through internal savings (see below). While improving local government, these changes can also be used by those who wish to argue that this central pressure and control is required for local government to perform. The scale and pace of this reform is recognised by those who are involved within it, and the chairman of the Audit Commission commented on the degree of excellence and rate of improvement in local government which in his view was rare to find elsewhere in both the public and the private sectors (Strachan 2004).

On the other hand, once all these efficiencies have been achieved and performance has improved, there remain few arguments left to central government as to why funding for local government should not be on a different basis. What appears to be emerging is a contractual relationship between local and central government and in some cases this is being extended into the wider public sector such as the establishment of Local Public Service Boards being piloted in Kent and Swindon. In their creation of a super public agency board for a locality, all public funding streams can be considered together for the first time. These boards are beginning to address not only the silos within local authorities, which have been reinforced by central government funding streams, but also the parallel approaches which apply in other agencies such as health, the police, and benefits support. The debates on *new localism* are concerned with just these issues.

Thus, the boundaries between central and local seem to be shifting in favour of the local. In many cases there has not been any consideration of the most effective levels of delivery for any benefit, scheme, or service. Some of these boundaries, both vertically and horizontally are being challenged, with the longer term outcome likely to be a 'territorial' and horizontal approach, a joined-up approach to finance and delivery within spatially defined administrative boundaries rather than vertical singular relationships between locality and the centre (CEC 2002; Morphet 2004b, 2004c; Stoker 2005). This issue was also added to the terms of reference of the Lyons Review of local government in September 2005 with the inclusion of the task of considering 'the current and emerging strategic role of local government in the context of national and local priorities for local services and the implications of this for accountability' (ODPM 2005f: PN 2005/0193).

The main shift is in the focus on the citizen and the locality away from the producer and the centre. But how is this to be achieved, and is it possible to define the likely role of finance in facilitating this shift?

The continuing legacy of the Layfield Committee

The Layfield Committee was set up as part of the last major raft of reviews and reforms of local government in the early 1970s, which coincided with the United Kingdom's entry to the EU. This was the last time when all these issues were considered together, although then, as now, they were seen as discrete activities. Only with hindsight is it possible to see the scale and range of the activity. The Layfield Committee (1976) was one of these major review processes and considered two specific principles concerning local authority funding. The first was that of equality between localities and any government action required to ensure this – that is, the principle of horizontal fiscal equalisation (HFE). Second, it considered the principles of taxation in the tiers of government and here it found a vertical fiscal imbalance, that is, the extent to which the principle of proximity between tax raising and expenditure was applied – in this case one tier of government raised taxation and had a duty to spend it (VFI). The Layfield Committee also viewed the relationship between raising taxation and transparency in its utilisation to be key. It proposed a form of local income tax which was seen as a pivotal way of reducing the VFI, although accepting with it some inherent inequality, that is, not entirely meeting the HFE principle.

These proposals were rejected at the time but have since continued to haunt the debate about local government funding. Stoker (2004, pp. 182–183) considers the legacy of Layfield through the use of four principles which he defines as transparency, justice in the distribution of resources, flexibility, and a holistic approach. In his discussion, Stoker relates each of these to the wider policy debate about the future of local government and its powers. Inevitably there are tensions between local discretion and a 'post-code lottery', not least given public experience and expectations in a centralised state. In other countries, such as the United States, these differences exist overtly and are seen to be part of the established system. The universality principle, which the post-1947 welfare state enshrined in U.K. public service delivery, leaves a different legacy. To some extent the differences in localities can be overcome by performance management and the adoption of base standards or 'floor targets' which have become increasingly common in their use. Thus, universal standards can be achieved with local citizens voting to pay for additional services.

The outstanding issue remains the disconnection between the raising of tax for the provision of local services through local government and the democratic oversight of this process. Further, the LGA argues that the proportion of public sector funding which is under direct democratic accountability at the local level, in which is included higher education, adult education and training, health, financial benefits, transport, and housing, is approximately only 30% (Bruce-Lockhart 2005), and that this situation should be changed to provide improved public trust and more efficient citizen-focused services. This is confirmed by other recent reviewers of the position. McLean and McMillan (2003, p. 9) point out that the United Kingdom have a 'substantial' VFI, which is seen to be problematic as it 'clouds responsibility and increases the incentives for fiscal irresponsibility' (p. 11), and they argue that the transfer of the business rate to a centralised system was a more painless way of increasing VFI than poll tax for example. Layfield's proposals for local income tax act remain a touchstone in many of these debates about local funding.

The dynamics of efficiency

One way of freeing up funding to be utilised by local discretion is the generation of savings within the organisation through efficiencies. Following the Gershon

Review (2004), local authorities were given 2.5% p.a. year-on-year efficiency targets from 2005 to 2008 with the savings being made available to deploy 'on the front line', that is, back into service delivery rather than administration. A number of areas for potential efficiency savings were identified in the Gershon Review including the procurement of goods and services and construction through the use of purchasing consortia and aggregated procurement processes. The local government efficiency agenda was supported through the establishment for Regional Centres of Excellence (RCEs), which were initially established for procurement purposes only but were quickly extended to include all activities which lead to excellent practice. These moves are paralleled by an increasing regionalisation of the approach to capacity building and performance in local government which has followed the outcome of CPA reviews through regional improvement partnerships.

The use of property assets – an example of improving efficiency at the local level

The Local Government Act 2003 gave local authorities new powers to fund improvements by borrowing money without government consent, as long as they could fund the debt. Restrictions on the use of capital finance by local authorities had been a major source of friction post-1979, and the ability of local authorities to manage the maintenance and repair of its estate had always been the subject of very tight financial control by the Treasury. Capital expenditure at the local level has always been viewed as part of national capital expenditure levels and limits. This approach has created a financial system unlike that in the private sector with no ability to make provision for maintaining or replacing fixed assets over time.

The 1998 White Paper on local government proposed some changes in the approach to capital financing with a move away from annual budgeting to one which was longer term and which could be related to the asset base of any local authority. The property asset base is often significant in the council's ability to manoeuvre in a financial crisis or its ability to hold down council tax levels if the income generated by property or other revenue streams can be used to offset at least part of the councils' running costs. In many cases this has motivated local authorities to sell their housing stock, creating significant capital injections. Another major factor has been the ability of councils to use certain funds in ways which give them freedom to spend in support of local need. Hence, car parking income and those generated by local authority land and property searches can be used for any local purpose and are not subject to equalisation in the same way as council tax. These funds have provided the means to provide for sports facilities, additional care and support for the elderly, and town centre enhancement schemes and are often overlooked as a means to support local community development.

The range of assets held by a local authority, particularly property, is a factor of history. In some cities such as Birmingham or Bath, the council purchased large amounts of land in the city centre or indeed developed the centre itself as in the case of Birmingham, which acquired much of the property when Chamberlain was Lord Mayor. These assets are now of considerable value. Other local authorities such as counties often have a land base of farms which were purchased in the 1930s as a means of securing the land against a depressed economy. Some councils have developed significant local assets such as airports, for example, Luton, Birmingham, and Manchester. Other local authorities have not built up or retained such portfolios and many urban and rural district councils were required to pass assets over the county or other authorities at the time of local government reorganisation in 1972–1974 and 1991–1997. At the same time, London and Metropolitan boroughs gained assets on the break up of the GLC and former metropolitan counties in 1985. Some councils pursued a programme of land acquisition, particularly before the 1960s, when the number of businesses and other business activities could make a significant local contribution to the assets of the local authority through the retention of the business rate income they generated.

The introduction of Asset Management Plans (AMPs) and the Single Capital Pot (SCP) were seen to be significant steps forward towards creating more positive management and maintenance of the capital assets held at the local level. However, this new approach was not to be confined to specific services and separate from the council's activities and priorities overall. Capital strategies for local authorities were to include

- Value and condition of assets
- Priorities and plans for local areas and partners
- Capital implications of service delivery plans (as part of local performance plans required under best value)
- Community needs and service priorities
- Key government policy objectives
- Funding opportunities (including linkages with the new deal for regeneration, European Union funds, the National Lottery and Public/Private Partnerships)
- Revenue implications of investment decisions
- Needs and contribution from business
- Accountability to the community. (DETR 1998, para. 9.11)

The preparation of AMPs has been taken as in 'in-house' activity with little specific inspection and examination of the process. Some local authorities now take a proactive approach to managing their property assets to promote regeneration or wider goals and now there seems to be a important link between land opportunities and major physical renewal such as that promoted through the Commonwealth Games in Manchester in 2002 and in London Olympic Bid for 2012. The public sector role in market renewal through its own property portfolio is now seen to be significant but the extent to which local authorities proactively manage their property assets varies.

A further new challenge is posed by the changing shape of the local authority workforce. Now many local authority staff use mobile working techniques to work in the field and many staff can work from home. Others are working jointly with public agencies and local authorities are frequently introducing multi-agency one-stop shops for local delivery. All of these changes point to a further review of the fitness of purpose of long-standing council accommodation for changing business requirements. Some local authorities such as Surrey County Council have developed area offices with work stations that can be used by staff members and increasingly local authorities are providing these facilities to allow staff to work in a more flexible way. This process may lead to a further major review of local authority property assets in the provision of accommodation for their own staff and re-provisioning with other agencies in order to generate improved service delivery and more efficiency.

The public service reform agenda is posing both challenges and opportunities for the local publicly owned asset base. In the Varney Review (Varney 2006) there are proposals for all local agencies to deliver their services from the same one-stop counters and to reduce their individual offices and service counters. Hence, local authorities could run post offices or be the location for a driving test while local authority services could be requested from GP surgeries in the future.

A new freedom – the case of business rates

The relationship between businesses and their local authority was seen to be a key feature of the rating system even after the introduction of the equalisation basis for local councils funding. The final break between the council and its business community on this form came in 1990 (Morphet and Brougham 1990) when the business rate was established as a separate fund known as the National Non-domestic Rate (NNDR). The proposals after the 1997 election recognised that this separation brought a potential weakness between these two interests in that businesses felt they had no stake in the local community as they could not see their contribution making any local difference. Proposals for improved consultation on the setting of the local council tax rate were seen to be one measure of change together with a discussion on how these locally generated finances were to be used but in effect an annual consultation did not provide a real means of re-establishing contact. The 1998 White Paper on local government floated a proposal for beacon councils to be able to set their own level of business rate but this was not pursued. This was followed by the green paper *Modernising Local Government Finance* (DTLR 2000). Business Improvement Districts (BIDs) were announced, and in 2003 a new initiative to allow a local authority to retain income generated from business rates was announced. This allowed additional income generated from business rates from businesses starting up or moving to the area to be retained by the local authority and used for its well-being.

These proposals have been welcomed, and other measures to improve business engagement at the local level have been implemented, such as membership of businesses of the LSPs and Neighbourhood Renewal initiatives but these are still not regarded as a means of restoring the basic relationship which prevailed until the reforms of 1990. Any such move to re-localise business rates is also rejected by the CBI as a retrogressive measure. The future policy direction on this issue is interesting particularly in the light of the newly emerging approach to generating national GDP through localities (HMT 2004b). This suggests a greater degree of common purpose and unanimity for the local economy than has hitherto been the case, which has been confirmed in the *Sub-national Review of Economic Development and Regeneration* (HMT 2007). In much of the debate on globalisation, the counter trend towards localisation, not least as a means of promotion sustainability and innovation, has been overlooked. The re-establishment of the direct relationship between business and local democracy could be effected by this changing direction of policy.

A new localist solution?

The studies of the future of local government finance continue. The Balance of Funding Review was included as a commitment in the local government White Paper 2001 and commenced in April 2003 for an anticipated year's work on the future of local government finance. As Wintour (2003a) points out, it could have been the most fundamental review of local government funding since the Layfield Review in 1976. The consultation paper raised a number of issues with the key ones being considered including

- various options for a full reform of council tax
- introduction of some form of local income tax
- the re-localisation of business rates
- the introduction of some new sources of revenue and/or the localisation of some central revenue schemes.

The Balance of Finding Review reported in July 2004, and its conclusion was that further more fundamental review was required, this time to be chaired by Sir Michael Lyons, former chief executive of Birmingham City Council. The terms of reference were published in October 2004:

What are the most pressing issues affecting the present system of local government funding? How might they be resolved, and what are the advantages and disadvantages of particular options? Who would be affected and how? In particular:

1 How should council tax best be reformed?
2 What is the case for providing local authorities with increased flexibility to raise a larger proportion of its funding locally, or additional revenue?

3   What other sources – including local income tax, reformed non-domestic rates and other local taxes and charges – could be used to raise supplementary revenue for local authorities? How would they work and what would be their advantages and disadvantages? Would a particular combination of options work better than others?
4   What are the implications for the financing of possible elected regional assemblies?
5   What are the priorities for analysis within the terms of reference? (Lyons 2004)

The Lyons Review provides an opportunity once again to consider local taxes, which may return as a key proposal some 30 years after the Layfield Committee first proposed it as a solution for local authority funding. The boundaries of what may be a local decision for funding and service standards may also have changed during the course of this debate and particularly since 1997. As Stoker (2004) points out, there is now public support for a more centrally directed set of standards in education although this is less clear in other service areas. Also, the extent to which local and national stands prevail in the community will depend on the level of service provision, its perceived quality, and the views of the service user. The issues in local funding have also been influenced by changes in funding for local authorities in Scotland and Wales. Following the Barnett formula (which was introduced in 1978 at the time of a failed devolution initiative), local authorities outside England have been funded to a higher level per capita and this difference has continued despite devolution. Indeed some of the policy choices made by the Scottish Parliament have increased resources to local authorities, for example, for older people and transport, although local taxation is also the subject of a specific review in Scotland which was announced in June 2004.

In line with the move to new localism in government, is there also a new localism approach to funding? McLean and McMillan (2003) argue that there is. They acknowledge that much of the government's localist 'talk' is undermined by its persistently centralist actions, which is constantly underscored by the application of targets, which then serve to skew local priorities. They argue that a more localist approach must be based on a principle of taxing locally and then suggest a variety of means of achieving this, including

1   reforming council tax and increasing the number of bands;
2   freedom for local authorities to raise congestion charges, to keep the funding and apply as they see fit;
3   remove restrictions on local authority borrowing powers;
4   nationalise the fire service;
5   give devolved administrations and regional assemblies the same tax powers as Scotland (i.e. to vary income tax by 3p in the pound);
6   return the business rate to local authorities;
7   introduce a land value tax;
8   transfer tax points to local and regional government (using the Canadian model).

104 Modern Local Government

It is perhaps this last model which is the most innovative as it leads to a restructuring of tax collection in the United Kingdom. In Canada, the federal government 'vacated' the collection of some of its cents in the dollar and allowed these to be collected by the provinces. These national and provincial taxes are collected together – sometimes nationally and sometimes locally, depending on the local regime. The improvement in e-government tools allows this to happen more easily than before, so some of the cost objections fall. It could also create considerable efficiency savings. McLean and McMillan (2003) suggest that there should be a new Territorial Grants Commission to oversee the distributive mechanism for local finance, with the same status as the Electoral Commission.

Others have also considered international approaches to local finance. Loughlin and Martin (2003) reviewed a range of models using the principles of 'own resources' that is funding which is generated through local taxation means and 'transfers' in funding from central government to structure their analysis. This review found that within Europe there has been an increase in the 'transfer' approach but that this had been accompanied by block grant systems, where local authorities are free to spend within an allocation and move away from ring fencing where the funding is tied to a specific purpose. However, Loughlin and Martin noted that there has also been an increased concern about this drift within Europe and identified some national attempts to restrict the volume of funding delivered through a 'transfer' approach. However, even within this scenario, Loughlin and Martin demonstrate that the position within the United Kingdom represents a higher proportion of funding 'transferred' than generated from 'own resources', where transfers account for 53% compared with 37% elsewhere in Europe on average.

Another model for central/local funding is the 'contractual' one, where local authorities are contracted to central government to delivery services to a specific base level, after which they can use their discretion in the ways in which they deliver beyond this. Another variant of this model is that of the franchise (Stoker 2004), which creates a tight control between central government and the local authority or franchisee. This approach would generate a 'vanilla' approach to local government, which would set specific service expectations by the centre and would reduce any local variants. As an approach, franchising offers a 'new universalism' in local government services, which would be an enhanced version of the central–local relations model which was used between 1979 and 1997. However, it would be difficult to work within a more localised and decentralised approach to the economy and democratic control of public funds and agencies.

Conclusions

Finance remains at the heart of the debate on the future of local governance of services in England. It was seen as the leading issue between central and local government in 1997 and remains so today. The future may lie in local income tax or in placing wider local public sector expenditure under local democratic control. Meanwhile, local authorities continue to use a widening range of powers and tools to extend the pool of their own funding which can be spent under their own decision-making powers and this is set to grow further. Is the future likely to be a contract between central and local government for the delivery of an agreed baseline of services, funded centrally together with a locally determined package which is funded through locally raised revenues from a variety of sources?

10

NEW LOCALISM

all chapter

Introduction

The notion of 'new localism' is one which has been at the heart of a growing debate in central and local government since 2002. The origins of 'new localism' derive from pressures on government to consider whether it should divest more central power to the local level. The first set of pressures came from the United States and is economic in its underlying drive. In studies such as that of Alesina and Spolaore (2003), which examines the relationship of the size of a country with its economic success, the premise has been that since 1945, a great number of smaller states have been created, which, given their size, are becoming more homogenous in their population characteristics. This homogeneity is leading to a more culturally concentrated market which becomes easier to serve in economic terms. This is a wider version of Putnam's notion of social capital, where a smaller state creates the community unity which he indicates leads to happier, more socially engaged and stable communities. Alesina and Spolaore also indicate that smaller states on the whole have smaller government structures (once their size is considered) which are also more efficient, less onerous on their citizens, and with more responsive ways in which they can act. Thus, an economically efficient future could be achieved through the adoption of smaller areas of governance as an organising principle. Smaller states are autonomous in government but join with other states for those activities which are most appropriate. This also supports an argument for regionalism within states. It also supports the larger world trading blocks such as the EU.

This interest in the size of government and the 'weight' it places on economic efficiency has also been a consistent theme in the United States since the Gore initiative to 'reinvent government' (Osborne and Gaebler 1992) as something smaller, more transparent, and customer led. This approach takes the view that 'central' government has become too large and is now hampering the economic health of the state. This notion has since developed further into a greater interest in the relationship between the scale of government and its performance. Better performance management could be a necessary prerequisite to 'letting go' and downsizing.

There are also economic arguments for smaller governance of smaller places coming from Europe. In the EU there is an additional economic imperative through the demographic problem facing states. Falling working age populations are needing to support a higher proportion of dependent, retired adults. If this demographic situation continues without any further action, it could generate higher labour costs, act as a disincentive for people to enter higher education, or encourage greater inward migration. A number of measures are being taken to address this concern including the encouragement and the subsequent enforced extension of working life so that a greater proportion of the population remains in the labour market. Another approach is to generate a labour shake out, and some EU member states such as France and Germany have introduced initiatives to support this policy. In England, much of the labour downsizing occurred in the private sector and in formerly owned public sector companies in the 1980s. However, the move to 'smaller' government could lead to both lower initial recruitment and a re-shaping of the public sector labour market so that people are available to enter other sectors to reduce the risk of the economy overheating. This approach is mirrored over the whole of Europe, although the EU also has the advantage of increased labour supply available from new member states to support a wider ageing population. These then create the economic principles for new localism.

There are other drivers for new localism within the EU which are political in character. Concerns about the low levels of electoral turnout in European parliamentary elections and the continuing debates about the nature of accountability, the 'democratic deficit', of its indirect political structures have encouraged a greater interest in focusing on the relationship between the EU and sub-national tiers of government, in particular regions and neighbourhoods, through the means of specific programmes which fund support at these levels.

The application of the principle of subsidiarity in the EU has primarily been regarded as a means of ensuring that the council of ministers and commission do not seek to remove powers from member state governments. At the same time, there has been an increasing drive to ensure that the principle is applied at the sub-national level (Loughlin 2001a). Since 1994, this has had a specific voice in the EU since the establishment of the Committee of the Regions. Loughlin (2001b) also argues that the emergence of a different relationship between the state and its sub-national levels through policies such as privatisation have also helped to build a more competitive approach between regions needing support, both within states and within the EU. Within the EU, it is also clear that regional economic performance is seen to be closely linked to regional identity, bringing the political and economic drivers more closely together. It is also now understood that the performance of any state in Europe can no longer be driven from the centre but has to be led from within the region and it is through this growth from the bottom up that the state and European economy will flourish (ODPM et al. 2004). The application of the principle of subsidiarity is also having other effects much as the review of devolved decision making which is taking place in the United Kingdom (HMT 2004b).

In all, locally based governance initiatives are being seen to be desirable across the world for a number of reasons:

- wider ownership of decision making
- increasing interest in voting thus improving the democratic accountability of decision making
- efficiency by reducing layers of bureaucracy
- effectiveness in delivery – smaller areas for delivery can provide more targeted approaches
- greater efficiency
- smaller government.

The rise of new localism

The notion of 'new localism' is, as Mulgan (2004) states, at times a confused one, or even a term which is used promiscuously (Corry et al. 2004). It first appeared as a concept in 2002 (Corry and Stoker 2003) in a pamphlet published by the New Local Government Network with a foreword by the former Chief Economic Adviser, Ed Balls. This was followed by a series of speeches from leading politicians. The notion of 'new localism' recognised that, since 1997, much has happened to change the quality and delivery of local government services. Change has also occurred in the way in which the democratic processes which govern delivery are arranged. In central government the initial key theme of 'joined-up government' has been replaced by the establishment of targets set within Public Service Agreements (PSAs) between the Treasury and individual government departments. Individual local authorities have also entered into LPSAs which have set stretch targets at the local level but these have had a far smaller effect than the requirements of central departments' to deliver their targets to the treasury. Where central departments are dependent on local delivery to ensure the achievement of their individual national targets in education, crime, and health, lack of integration has a fundamental effect on what happens at the local level. It is this issue which dominated the debate about public service reform in the second term of the Labour government during 2001–2005.

There are those who also make a strong case for the impact of the 'local'. As Quirk (2001) indicates, technology has made a considerable difference to the world and the way much of it is able to conduct its affairs:

> But these trends have not led, for the majority of people, to the death of distance or the loss of locality. Closer events have the biggest influence upon us. And, for each of us, local, locale and locality still matter more than global and universal. (Quirk 2001, p. 1)

There are further dimensions to this debate. Corry (2003) has set the dilemma of local improvement of delivery within the context of the Blair–Brown debate about the future. He describes three elements of this discussion. The first is the extent to which the centre can adequately 'direct' local performance. On this point, Corry argues that both sides are agreed that a more local approach, similar to older style municipalism, is the way forward, even although this will lead to differences at the local level. Against this, Corry indicates, are those who would wish to identify targets that can be achieved rather than different targets between localities. The establishment of national targets on specific health or social conditions need different approaches at the local level. Although understood by bodies advising government, this subtlety is yet to be fully understood within the policy community although perhaps more familiar to those with experience of delivery. This approach would still allow for some differences at the local level in addition to the achievement of minimum standards.

The second issue identified by Corry is related to competition and choice. Here Corry argues that the Treasury is in favour of competition for main providers, through PFI or other means. However, Corry defines the alternate view as one where competition is offered at the point of delivery for people in areas of poor service delivery. This was characterised as the Millburn position in health (Milburn 2003) and the debates on health markets through foundation hospitals. Added to this is a debate about how funding should be raised, with the Treasury being concerned to maintain a tight grip on raising funds, particularly in health. However, it is interesting to note that the powers for local authority trading, contained in the Local Government Act 2003 provide some alternate means to generate additional revenue, while the latter period of 2003 was dominated by a debate on public fines – whether they are more important to deter behaviour such as speeding or avoiding vehicle tax duty or whether that would have a more impor- tant role in generating income for the Treasury, the police, or local authorities.

The third point raised by Corry is the level of democratic accountability over those on the front line. The Treasury is characterised as wanting that power to be exercised by frontline managers without recourse to local democratic accountability thus centralising by default. The proposals for local boards in health, education, and in police management made by Blears (2003) are seen as important tools for those wanting to meet the spirit of the movement of services to the neighbour- hood or 'front line' while still retaining a very clear line of accountability to the department and minister who controls the funds. In a system where individual departmental targets remain, this seems an almost inevitable consequence – perhaps an unintended outcome – but a result nevertheless of weighting specific performance over more integrated outcomes. Blears argues for a more active citizenry, which is more interested in specific service delivery rather than general political engagement. As the government is organised in departments with themed functions, any pressure for change needs to be targeted on the silos where power is currently located. If central government was organised differently, pressure may be applied in different ways to change priorities and decisions for resource allocation – the fundamental goal of community (and all other) politics.

The principle of new localism is being implemented, but beneath the banner heading there is contested space, with much more at stake than the future of local government. New localism within the package of post-1997 constitutional reforms – devolution, reform of the House of Lords, judicial reform, voting, reform of the House of Commons – is a change to create potential parity between local and central governance. The view that effective economic and social delivery needs different forms of governance is critical to this agenda. At the same time there will be many who do not welcome the structural and cultural changes that such approaches will bring. As all those involved in change management appreciate, the ability of the *status quo* to exert the great force of inertia is often underestimated. At best what happens is partial reform and implementation. What is interesting about this package of reforms which support the broad notion of new localism is the scale and number of institutions involved. It could also lead to a more executive style of government where working for a common cause both strategically and locally may emerge as the expected norm.

Local government is, therefore, the major beneficiary from the application of the principle of new localism. It may not receive all the local freedoms whilst there are concerns about 'post-code lotteries' in the delivery of services. At the same time, the new degrees of freedom may be as great as those anticipated 1997 but hardly expected in the 'best-value' years. The developing governance structures may also be an amalgam of all the approaches proposed. At the sub-local authority level, local involvement in dealing with locality based improvement is critical for its success, and elections to neighbourhood development groups have attracted much higher turnouts than local elections. The means to achieve neighbourhood working exist either from the Local Government Act 2000 or the application of new town and parish councils. Directly elected single-purpose boards might also have a role in this kind of structure.

At the local level, the emergence of the Local Public Service Boards (Kent County Council 2003; Corry et al. 2004) command support as a means of moving forward. Not only do they provide the means of overcoming the problems generated by silo public services for the individual, community, or company, but they can also create significant back office savings through back office systems, staff, and premises.

A further version of the new localism is the 'pluralist model' proposed by Corry et al. (2004) which suggests benefits could be provided while minimising the problems of delivery between agencies at the local level. Corry et al. set these against the opposites of silo and municipal structures. The pluralist approach seems difficult to understand unless taken to mean adopting differing approaches at each level – the Local Public Service Board at local authority level and pluralist, perhaps more single-service-based approaches at neighbourhood level although the authors do not make this distinction in their proposals. The model may be considered a 'fudge' not to upset either central or local government. Corry et al. (2004) support more sub-authority devolution although not with the sense of clarity which may be needed for successful implementation.

If new localism is to be the means of improving both local democracy and local delivery for the benefit of all, it will need some different operating principles from those that have gone before. Different incentives will need to be applied which relate to outcomes and delivery in a joined-up way rather than specific PSA targets.

Place shaping

In May 2006 the delivery of new localism in practice was re-branded as place shaping by Sir Michael Lyons in a report from his inquiry into local government. Entitled *National Prosperity, Local Choice and Civic Engagement: A New Partnership between Central and Local Government for the 21st Century* (Lyons 2006), the report applies a practical form of the subsidiarity principle for local government. In this report, for the first time, Lyons attempts to define what local authorities are there to do and the powers and resources that they need to undertake this task. Lyons moves away from an unplanned and haphazard history of the delivery of services by local and central government as determined by governing legislation to a more systematic view of what are the respective roles of central and local government. This is a new approach and one that is coalesced around place – not surprisingly perhaps as local authorities are now defined more by their spatial boundaries than the legal boundaries to their powers that existed in 1997.

Lyons proposes that place shaping should include

1 building and shaping local identity;
2 representing the community, including in discussions and debates with organisations and parts of government at local, regional and national level;
3 regulating harmful and disruptive behaviours;
4 maintaining the cohesiveness of the community and supporting debate within it, ensuring that smaller voices are heard;
5 helping to resolve disagreements, such as over how to prioritise resources between services and areas, or where new housing and development should be located;
6 working to make the local economy more successful, to support the creation of new businesses in the area, including through making the area attractive to new investment and skilled workers, and helping to manage economic change;
7 understanding local needs and preferences and making sure that the right services are provided to local people through a variety of arrangements including collective purchasing, commissioning from suppliers in the public, private and voluntary sectors, contracts or partnerships and direct delivery; and
8 working with other bodies to respond to complex challenges such as national disasters or other emergencies. (Lyons 2006, para. 3.2)

The notion of place shaping and all that it comprises was included in the local government white paper, Strong and Prosperous Communities 2006, although more was said on the local government leadership role than the devolution of local service leads from central government.

Pressures for reductions in local power

There are a number of underlying trends which support further autonomy for local government while others are strongly pulling at greater centralisation. At the same time as the pressures for increasing local governance have been growing, the insertion of a neighbourhood and parish tier is seen to be creating an alternative power base to be used by government departments that wish to circumvent local authorities (Blears 2003; Beecham 2005; ORPM 2005c). Those who argue against an increased role of local authorities cite a number of key reasons for the inherent 'riskiness' of such an approach.

Low voter turnout

The perceived loss of the democratic mandate is used as the primary argument for reducing local powers. Low voter turnout and the marginal success of the use of new voting methods to increase citizen engagement are seen of evidence of an approach which has now lost credibility. If local elections are seen to be a judgement on central government then there may be reasons for increasing central–local alignment. On the other hand, local democracy has been shown to be more alive where local issues are taken forward, although there is a strong argument that this only works at the neighbourhood level, which is a point made by those in favour of a more centralist approach (Blears 2003).

Targetry

Targetry drives central government departments to deliver their PSAs from the Treasury's Comprehensive Spending Review process and their Five-year Plan requirements from the Cabinet Office. One of the areas where targetry is seen to be most active since 1997 has been in education policy and delivery. The public promises made by central government have traditionally been the delivery responsibility of local government. In the period since 1997, the separateness of the local educational authority and the 'handcuffs' on funding commonly known as 'passporting' have served to generate some of the greatest debates in the changed status of local government. When this is coupled with distinctive and separate performance inspections, this tension increases. As Bache (2003) states,

> This enthusiasm for greater cross-sectoral involvement, alongside the desire of the centre to retain control over its highest priority policy, highlights a paradox at the

heart of contemporary politics: how the centre governs in the context of governance. (p. 300)

Additionally, Stoker argues that although the ODPM (then the DETR) was more focused on a bottom-up approach, this was not the same for other departments (Stoker 1999) who were reluctant to abandon top-down regulatory styles of relationship.

Failure

Local authorities have been seen to be too risky and it is frequently argued that local authorities are not sufficiently capable of being able to deliver on the central agenda, not least as it has been set out since 1997. This has been a particular concern of departments dealing with education, crime and disorder, and social care. However, the new inspection regimes and the implementation of the CPA regime have started to demonstrate a measurable improvement in performance. Unified performance assessment regimes have also illuminated the silo nature of departmental inspections, where two different departments can be using similar or competing measures of success. However, over time, the argument has shifted to the issue of whose failure is at risk. As local authorities are seen to be improving in their performance, central departments continue to argue that their own targets are at risk through local failure to deliver. Departmental targets are being increasingly moved to whole life and whole locality approaches in the 2007 Spending Review. Departments will need to work together and with partners including local government to receive funding.

Continuing suspicion

Despite a reform programme for local government which was started in 1997 there are as many differences in opinion in Whitehall and Westminster in the future direction for local government as there were before this process commenced:

> there is little agreement in Whitehall and Westminster about the future of local government in Britain. Ministers and civil servants (and their immediate successors) have views as individualistic and developed as any other group. The diversity is perhaps surprising given the amount of legislation and debate on the subject during the past twenty years. (Jones and Travers 1996, p. 103)

The lack of a coherent approach is seen to be a strong weakness in the future direction of local government. In the Strategic Audit of the United Kingdom (Cabinet Office 2003) some bold statements are made about local government and its future. In s. 5.2, the strategic audit states that in settling the balance between national government regions and local government (in s. 5.2),

[d]evolution to Scotland, Wales and London has been a success. Regional government in parts of England is now being considered.

However, major challenges remain, particularly in relation to local government:

1 UK local democracy is weak in comparative terms – the huge gap with national election is unique. Turnout is low and falling further.
2 The performance of councils varies hugely – they represent some of the most and least innovative parts of the public sector. Services have improved since 1997 but at a very slow rate.
3 Our lowest tier of local government is unusually large and current local government structures are based in part on unfounded assumptions about economies of scale.

At the very local level: citizens identify strongly with local neighbourhoods; street level issues are growing in political salience.
IA number of key choices need to be resolved
On regions:

• What role could regional assemblies play?

On local government:

1 A shared view is needed across Whitehall (and local government itself) of the purpose and role of local government – conflicting views are impeding reform and improvement.
2 What is the appropriate tax base at the local level?
3 Central government needs to decide whether to mandate a limited number of national floor standards in key services areas (and accept more local variation)
4 Choices need to be made about whether to extend the accountability of other key local services – in particular police and primary care trusts.

At the very local level

• There may be a need to build up new neighbourhood bodies that would be responsible for issues such as local public space. (Cabinet Office 2003, s. 5.2, pp. 106–107)

Culture and habit

The cultural differences between central and local government remain at the heart of much of the distrust between the two. To central government, local government is seen to be fractured – too difficult to comprehend and understand, and local politicians are not held in high regard. The 'fractured' local government argument is also used by the private sector which would prefer to deal with larger organisations and have fewer contracts. Central government and the civil service have always seen their strength in policy and legislation, leaving other agencies and local government to deliver.

One issue which remains a concern is the poor level of respect in the relationship between the civil service and local government. Stewart has coined the phrase 'elite contempt' to describe how the civil service views local government. There have been some studies around this relationship but perhaps not as many as might be expected. As Flinders (2002, p. 32) states, 'officials place more emphasis on avoiding mistakes and protecting their minister . . . this defensive disposition is preserved throughout civil service training'. This means that devolving any responsibility may lead to consequences which cannot be 'controlled' or 'managed'.

However, since 1997, there has been a rising objective of delivery in central government policy making and legislation. Delivery is where local authorities have been seen to be more experienced and successful. Central government has brought many former local authority officers into various roles to lead mainstream work while the prime minister has also established the Prime Minister's Delivery Unit (PMDU) with the aim of ensuring that policies are translated into deliverable solutions which are focused on outcomes. In the longer term, central government has realised that it may need less 'policy making' as it concentrates more on delivery and also devolves policy making to the local level (Lyons 2006).

At the same time, local government's view of central government has begun to change although trust is not strong. Through the development of closer working relationships, fostered in part by the Central Local Partnership (CLP) established in 1997, there is now a formal means of raising problems and proposals. The CLP has also created many sub-organisations promoting change through specific initiatives. However, trust remains a key issue in two main areas. The first is finance and there is a recognition that local authorities are underfunded and that this needs to be addressed (Audit Commission 2003d). Local financial autonomy is seen to be the goal and despite several attempts this issue is still far from being resolved. The second is the ability of central government to control its departments and bring a more coherent approach to its own work. There have been some reforms but many local authorities are not yet convinced that the transfer of local lead for the negotiations of the new LAAs (ODPM 2005a) to the Government Offices (GO) will bring forward the degree of coordination required, particularly as GOs are not seen to be 'big hitters' in the Whitehall village.

At the same time, it can suit local authorities to have central departments issuing requirements and standards. This may mean that local authorities can argue to their communities that they have 'no choice' about expenditure priorities as these have been set centrally. Similarly, local authority officers can use the same arguments with their councillors. Reductions in central requirements and more local financial autonomy will lead to a new relationship between the local authority and its communities, which may have effects at the ballot box. At the same time, the local agenda for priority and action is being set through the LSP (ODPM/LGA 2003; ODPM 2005e) and the increased expectation of the use of evidence-based policy making at the local level which may provide a means for supporting specific spending priorities. In the longer term the bringing together of the public budget at the local level will increase transparency of action and expenditure and make it more susceptible to democratic leadership.

Conclusions

When 'new localism' first emerged, there were few who believed that it would have any influence on the structure of the local–central state. Developments since then have demonstrated that new localism has been applied with more to come. The implementation of CAA and self/peer review in 2008 is a far cry from the BV regime in 1997. In 10 years, the trust in local authority delivery has moved from a central to a decentralised model which includes within it other local public service bodies.

LOCAL STRATEGIC PARTNERSHIPS – THE WAY FORWARD

Introduction

Local authorities have been working with other public, private, and voluntary agencies in their localities for many years. This way of working has been both formal and informal. Local authorities have often found ways of crossing organisational and institutional boundaries to overcome problems in delivery for places and people. However, where partnership working has been less successful, there has often been public concern about those people or problems that slip between organisations. In other instances, numerous initiatives are aimed at the same community or target group represent bureaucracy and duplication. More recently, there have been concerns that many of the government's schemes for individual agencies or local authorities are too narrowly focused and do not allow wider issues or flexibilities in working with the local dimension of problems. This chapter considers the approach to partnership working at the local level which has emerged since 1997 and its onward direction which could help to shape the future of local governance.

Partnership working – programmes and policies

The use of the term 'partnership' working in local government has been utilised at least since 1978 when the Inner City Partnerships were announced. These approaches followed rather different models of area-based working which were characterised by the Community Development Projects (Benington et al. 2006). These early approaches to working directly with communities to overcome fundamental problems of poverty and unemployment were seen to be important but in the end they did not lead to effective mainstreaming into the work of the constituent agencies nor did they have any lasting effect on government policies or indeed on the private sector interests in localities. Further policy development in the 1980s and the 1990s also led to attempts to encourage local agencies to work together on the ground particularly through the utilisation of soft funding streams and bidding processes. These covered schemes for urban areas, such as several rounds of Single Regeneration Budgets (Imrie and Raco 2003), and in rural areas, local programmes have been funded by LEADER, the EU's rural initiative.

The introduction of multi-governance and multi-agency working was boosted following the United Kingdom's membership of the EU. The approach to programme-based schemes, led by government regional offices, with a mixed management group, representing the communities which were being served, although without delegation of funding decisions, have a marked character from 1973 onwards. They parallel the development of the EU's approach to targeted area-based support to deal with social exclusion as part of its wider structural and regional policies.

In 1997 the effectiveness of these multilayered approaches was reconsidered by the incoming government. This found that approaches were often competitive and contradictory with schemes designed to serve the same population group frequently having mutually oppositional targets. The early work of the Social Exclusion Unit (SEU) and more integrated 'joined-up approaches' were trailed in order to develop a more holistic approach to citizen needs. A number of other 'joining-up' experiments were also commenced at this time such as the Crime and Disorder Reduction Partnerships (CDRPs) which were implemented in 1998–1999 and the various action zones such as those for education or health which provided sources of funding for small areas available after competition between localities. Yet another approach was the establishment of Sure Start schemes which brought together a number of agencies in a locality to support children and families of preschool children, based on the assumption that this was an important part of ensuring improved life chances for these children. Other partnerships were developed to bring together service delivery such as Youth Offending Teams and programmes to deal with delayed discharges of older people from hospitals into local authority care, colloquially known as 'bed-blocking syndrome'.

After 1997, further initiatives were deployed to break down the departmental and agency silos which existed. The use of the PAT formula for social exclusion, through which the government brought together a cross-section of people to sit in a taskforce to consider the barriers to supporting specific groups of disadvantaged people or neighbourhoods, was one means that was pursued during this period (Morphet 2003a). Another was the use of the Cabinet Office Policy and Innovation Unit to undertake cross-cutting studies, for example, on Better Policy Delivery and Design (2001).

Although these approaches were targeting different age groups and communities to improve a joined-up approach, they were often area or neighbourhood specific. They were also frequently based on a 'we are the worst' approach in making a case for funding. They helped to retain a dependency culture within local authorities where there were no incentives to make improvements in life chances or to reduce other negative indices, as improved outcomes would lead to a reduction in additional funding for schemes and a lower grant settlement each year.

There were also changes in the policy climate in the EU. Enlargement in 2004 led to a significant review of the financial arrangements which would need to be in place. Area-based funding for dealing with regeneration and social exclusion through a variety of EU programmes had largely been spent on infrastructure, and there were mixed results. This policy climate had been changing since the early 1990s, but by the end of the decade, more inclusive-based local programmes were emerging from Brussels. These approaches were becoming manifest in different ways – through mega-regional, inter-regional, urban, rural, and neighbourhood programmes. A move away from targeting specific localities to 'edge to edge' approaches supported by a programmed approach was beginning to emerge in an overarching framework of 'territorial cohesion'.

This broader approach brought with it a number of changes not least in the ways in which it influenced U.K. policy thinking. At its heart was the expectation that local authorities should take a wider view about the whole of their area, on the assumption that there would be variances in service performance and life chances exhibited in different ways at the neighbourhood level. There was also an assumption that public sector funding could be better utilised through reducing some of the fixed costs associated with a high degree of fragmentation in service provision and reusing these funds in direct service delivery. There were also concerns about the continuing sense of competition or even unintended consequences of actions between local agencies, sometimes propelled by their parent government departments seeking to maximise their performance without always considering the implications elsewhere.

Local Strategic Partnerships

The ability of councils to promote the economic, social, and environmental well-being of their area without recourse to the need for further legal powers was a significant step forward in dealing with these issues. The second was to allow local authorities to supply services to any other organisation. Both provisions were contained in the Local Government Act 2000. Also, within the act was a duty for each local authority to prepare a Community Strategy which embodied the community's approaches to dealing with these issues on the ground. Outside the legal framework, local authorities were also encouraged to establish LSPs, which were mandatory in the 88 areas receiving Neighbourhood Renewal Funding (NRF) through the Government's Offices for the Regions (GOs). By 2004, virtually all local authorities had introduced an LSP – and these have a programme of action for joint working between all or some of their partners at the local level. LSPs do not have a specific legal basis, although this is proposed (DCLG 2006) and are expected to be accompanied by a duty for local public bodies to cooperate in the process.

The ability of local authorities to enter into partnerships was included in the Local Government Act 2000, s. 2(4), as a power for local authorities to

- incur expenditure
- give financial assistance to any person
- enter into arrangements or agreements with any person
- co-operate with or facilitate or co-ordinate the activities of any person
- exercise on behalf of any person any functions of that person
- provide staff, goods or services, or accommodation to any person.

The guidance from government indicated that the LSP would be a 'single body' that

1 brings together at a local level the different parts of the public sector as well as the private, business, community and voluntary sectors so that different initiatives and services support each other and work together;
2 is a non-statutory, non-executive organisation;
3 operates at a level which enables strategic decisions to be taken and is close enough to individual neighbourhoods to allow actions to be determined at community level; and
4 should be aligned with local authority boundaries. (DETR 2001c, para. 1)

The guidance went on to suggest that the LSP should be the local 'partnership of partnerships' – the point where all the other plans and partnership initiatives should be brought together. In terms of leadership of the LSP, the guidance indicated that 'members of the LSP should decide who should take the lead' (DETR 2001c, para. 11). The GO was also expected to be connected to all LSPs. The organisations expected to be considered for LSP membership were extensive and were included in an annexe to the guidance as were examples of potential LSP structures.

In 2001, *A New Commitment to Neighbourhood Renewal – National Strategy Action Plan* was published (DTLR 2001b), and in those areas designated for receipt of NRF, LSPs were required to be accredited by their regional GO. Accreditation will depend on LSPs demonstrating that

1 they are effective, representative and capable of playing a key strategic role;
2 they actively involve all key players, including the public, private, community and voluntary sectors;

3 they have established genuine common local priorities and targets and agreed actions and milestones leading to demonstrable improvements against measurable baselines;

4 members have aligned their performance management systems, criteria and processes to that of the LSP;

5 they reduce not add to the bureaucratic burden; and

6 they build on best practice from successful partnerships by drawing on experiences of regional structures and national agencies. 6 (DETR 2001c, para 2.6)

The establishment of LSPs has caused many issues to be raised. Local authority political leaders have never been content with the ambiguity of LSPs. As the main democratic body within the community, they have taken the view that leadership should automatically be conferred on the local authority rather than left for the LSP to determine and this was proposed in 2005 (ODPM 2005e). Through subsequent CPA assessments, local authorities are more systematically assessed on their partnership working through the LSP than any of the other constituent bodies such as the police or health which have the same requirements to work in this way.

Within the partnership structures of local authorities, long-established working arrangements were also seen to be threatened. Most local authorities already had good partnership working in some areas such as crime reduction, tourism, or working with young people. The imposition of the LSP was seen to undermine this work and potentially to destabilise it. Some LSPs have overcome these fears through the establishment of a super LSP board which brings together only very few of the key partners to provide leadership leaving all the other arrangements intact (e.g. Croydon, Blackburn with Darwen). Another concern has been the potential for translating the LSP into a corporate body which can make executive decisions and employ staff.

How are LSPs developing?

The development of LSPs has been supported in a variety of ways particularly through the establishment of networks and learning sets including one on governance. This has identified a number of the key issues which can help or hinder progress (ODPM 2004i). These include considering explicitly the tensions between elected councillors and other representatives on the LSP. They also identify four key models for LSP working, which are 'advisory, commissioning, laboratory and community empowerment' and suggest that the alignment between understanding the role of the LSP and its governance is fundamental, and 'governance arrangements have to match' (p. 9). The guidance demonstrates that in each of the four types of LSP it is important to recognise the different roles of each of the representatives whether they be councillors, the voluntary sector, or from business and the differences in rules of engagement which are shown below.

Advisory	Commissioning	Laboratory	Community empowerment
• Rules about attendance	• Transparency about how decisions are made	• Rules should be minimal	• Clear expectations
• How to get things on the agenda	• Financial powers	• Freedoms and permissions	• Responsibilities
• How meetings are organised	• Legal powers	• Ground rules	• Networking and communication
• Advance notice of items	• Accountability	• Mutual understanding and respect	• Measures of success
• Roles and responsibilities	• Conflicts of interest or probity	• Safe space	• Behaviour conflict resolution
• Membership	• Clarity of purpose or function	• Self-facilitating	• Rules about representation and process
• Protocols about behaviour	• Boundaries		
	• Delegation of authority		

Source: ODPM (2004g, p. 13).

In order to assess the development of LSPs, a 5-year action research programme from the Warwick Business School was commissioned to track progress. One of the factors assessed in the Warwick research was the extent to which LSPs which have been in receipt of NRF may have varied from those which have not had a share in this £88m. pot. Others have also been looking at this issue including Liddle and Townsend (2003). In their study of two LSPs in receipt of NRF, they found that a number of the expected concerns in establishing partnership working were present. In particular, it had been difficult to engage the private sector and also for those in the voluntary and community sector to give up their time to engage even with financial support from the Community Empowerment Fund set up for this purpose. Liddle and Townsend (2003, p. 41) conclude that LSPs can be left with the 'usual suspects', who are already involved in organisations which receive funding and who can 'crowd out prospective newcomers'. They also found that 'officials' from local and central government and public agencies can still dominate membership. Although a useful tool, the accreditation process has also been found to have some drawbacks, with LSPs being driven by those whom the GO see 'in a good light' (Liddle and Townsend 2003, p. 41) even if they may have vested interests.

A factor which may contribute to the success of any LSP is the length of time for which it has been functioning albeit under other names and guises. Geddes (2004) found that it can take up to 7 years to develop a mature working style and Liddle and Townsend (2003) quote the success of the East Durham LSP which had at least a 10-year history, managing EU programmes for funding in the coalfields. However, even with this legacy, it is still difficult to assess progress as many LSPs are still at the vision and target setting stages which preceded the estsblishment of the LSP.

Another concern is the potential misfit between the representatives of different organisations and the importance of the issue to the locality. Liddle and Townsend (2003) report that GOs and regional bodies send relatively junior members of staff to the LSP, who may not be able to bring forward the backing of their whole organisation. The partnership may also be working together for collaborative advantage rather than for other reasons (Apostolakis 2004), although specific relationships may be both dysfunctional and unequal as this research found in the Leicester LSP.

Finally work has been undertaken to assess the best ways of mainstreaming the work of LSPs so that projects can be taken into programmes rather than project funded and was developed by an Action Learning Sets (ODPM 2004j). This identified key components of successful mainstreaming:

- Collection and pooling of information on patterns of resource use
- Developing a shared vision and identifying priorities for community outcomes
- Strategic review of options for realignment of resources
- Facilitation of change
- Learning and dissemination of results across partners
- Reconciliation of tensions between individual organisational accountabilities and collective responsibilities to the LSP, and unblocking when tensions arise. (ODPM 2004j, p. 4)

The practice of pooling budgets was seen to be particularly important to share both in the vision and in the outcomes of implementation.

How effective are LSPs so far?

A continuing issue in the assessment of the success of LSPs is the ability to measure their effective performance, the 'difference' which they make in their localities. One approach has been to examine ways in which performance indicators can be integrated across LSPs in order to assess their effectiveness at developing approaches which can make a difference in outcomes at the local level. As part of the on-going research into the effective development of LSPs commissioned by ODPM, a study undertaken by OPM (2003) has shown that there are some specific ways used by LSPs which have been able to start to tie together activities and outcomes in measurable ways. The study concludes that successful outcomes depend on the centrality of performance management for the LSP, which can generate 'evidence' of results (OPM 2003, p. 3) on which to consider future actions. The study advises against using this performance management approach to further micro-manage local agencies but rather 'over time, the LSP needs to develop a performance management framework that will enable partners to monitor, evaluate and plan joint work in such a way that they are held to account for their individual actions and achieve better results collectively than they would by working alone' (p. 4).

Other studies have considered the effectiveness of partnership governance structures using governance assessment tools specifically derived for the purpose (e.g. Mathur et al. 2004). The assessment of governance not only finds that it has to incorporate all the tensions and inconsistencies that are inherent in partnership working but also to find those who through their roles or personalities can provide leadership to overcome these. There are also issues around the sense of integration or detachment which partnership members choose to exert with their own sponsoring organisations. Although representing specific bodies and, in some cases, being expected to commit them to action through partnership decisions, not all partnership members establish these links. Sometimes partnership members can 'go native' and prefer to support the agenda of the partnership above that of their own organisation and do not undertake the continuing transmission of issues and decisions in both directions. It is also the case that some sponsoring organisations, including local authorities, will nominate to external bodies those representatives who can be most disruptive in their own work. Engaging the time and energy of a councillor or a committee member in an external body can ensure that internal workings of the sponsoring organisation run more smoothly. This can work to the advantage of the nominating organisation although there are problems for the partnerships which could have a majority of representatives nominated for this reason.

In managing any organisation which is run by representatives, there are always concerns at the extent to which nominated representatives take responsibility and feel accountability for the decisions which they take and any services which are to run. This can be equally true in organisations which have public nominees on a board as a partnership. As Liddle and Townsend (2003) found, this can generate more power for the secretariat whose task it is to progress the business of the partnership. Another outcome of this approach is that the partnership never takes decisions to 'act' but rather to cooperate or to work towards the same objectives, which can be non-specific and may lead to little progress. The extent to which any sector can participate in partnership working will depend on its own resources and the salience of the partnership's issues for its own intersts. Representatives from the voluntary and business sectors are likely to have their own interests not least where financial survival is generally the highest priority for both types of organisation. Partnership working may only be a high-value task where it enables the organisation to generate more funding or fewer conflicts. For a business, understanding the community in which it works may make it easier to progress with change, although this may not be an issue for the smallest or largest companies which may have other concerns on their agendas. For the community sector, much advice and research has been published which demonstrates the ways in which these relationships may be improved (e.g. Home Office, n.d., pp. 1–4).

Partnership working is always challenging and can often be the most difficult way of working at the local level. Some partnerships are 'required' to work together in order to access funds. Even if the partners are committed to the general objectives and the vision is shared, there may be many different approaches to achieving these ends. The differences in styles and approach for delivery are often considerable and may be related to the degree of funding and support available to individual partners. For local authorities or health agencies, the partnership may reflect their interest in meeting some central targets or objectives, although it is often true for health and the police that locally determined priorities can be in conflict with those set by central government departments. These tensions have to be resolved locally by operational managers.

The future for LSPs, LAAs, and Public Service Boards?

The role of LSPs has continued to develop and evolve to one which is now central to the future consideration of local government. There are two specific ways in which this is being pursued. The first was through LPSAs in their second iteration introduced in 2004 as LAAs (ODPM/LGA 2003). The second was through a proposal for 'LSPs with teeth', that is, public service boards were made by the excellent councils' Innovations Forum in 2003 (Blackburn with Darwen 2003; Kent County Council 2003; LBHF 2003; Peterson 2004). LSPs are now seen to be expressing their priorities and programmes for action through Community Strategies, identifying the ways in which they will deal with the most difficult issues locally through LAAs and are seeking a joined-up approach to pool local public agency funding within an area from welfare payments, policy, health, and local government. This approach has been demonstrated by Kent County Council, which aims at a

> new, ultra-lightweight but focussed vehicles to take responsibility for improving the delivery of local public service outcomes at a local level which strengthens the horizontal links between main public services, without diluting the formal accountability through Ministers to Parliament and without provoking the need for distracting reorganisations and transfers of functions. (Kent County Council 2003, p. 2)

The main focus of this approach is to integrate delivery between agencies where there are differing targets and operational modes. These are particularly difficult issues at the point where two agencies are caring for the same individual or where the individual passes from the care of one to another, such as in social care or support for parents in work. Kent proposes that the arrangements should last for 3 years, would require no additional powers as this could be achieved within the Local Government Act 2000, and should be under the management of a newly created LPSB.

The Audit Commission has also been reviewing ways in which LSPs and more locally joined-up working could be more successfully pursued. In their study *People, Places and Prosperity* (2004a), the Audit Commission demonstrates that the continuing separation of streams of funding and objectives serve to undermine joined-up working at the local level and that this is still having a deleterious effect on communities. They found that the promotion of economic, social, and environmental well-being was more likely to be successful where national and local priorities are 'fully aligned and where local partners achieve coherence in establishing their priorities and targets' (p. 2). The continuing number of partnership arrangements and funding streams which still exist, despite the introduction of LSPs, are still seen to hamper delivery at the local level, and this is supported by other research (Buck et al. 2002). These partnerships seem to be primarily engaged in attracting short-term project funding which makes mainstreaming and long-term planning more difficult. However, the Audit Commission did not suggest that the LSPs should be replaced but rather they should strengthened to become the basis of LAAs.

The government has responded to the Audit Commission's proposals with two approaches. The first is the publication of *Local Area Agreements: A Prospectus* (ODPM 2004k) and the second is an invitation to contribute to the consideration of *The Future of Local Government: Developing a 10 Year Vision* (ODPM 2004l). In the ministerial foreword to the prospectus, LAAs are described as representing 'a radical new approach to improve co-ordination between central government and local authorities and their partners, working through the Local Strategic Partnership' (ODPM 2004l, p. 5). The key components remain much the same as in earlier partnership working and are stated as

- simplified funding for Safer and Stronger communities
- strengthened Local Public Service agreements
- strengthened national strategy for Neighbourhood renewal
- a stronger role for Government Offices
- pilot local area agreements. (ODPM 2004l, p. 7)

The LAAs are proposed to have a series of key themes around specific groups and communities which are already identified in the jointly agreed priorities for local and central government (CLP 2000). Between 2005 and 2009 these are in 'blocks' – including children and young people, safer and stronger communities, healthier communities and older people, and local regeneration – which have been negotiated separately and brought together into a single LAA. From 2009 a 'single pot' for funding in a locality with no barriers between different public sector budgets and funding streams, with greater local flexibility in order to address local needs will be implemented. The second is to further rationalise the separate locally based funding initiatives which run in parallel to bring these into the LAA. All unitary and county councils were included in the LAA programme in 2005.

The effectiveness of delivery is seen to be assessed in a number of ways including proposed Local Area Profiles developed by the Audit Commission and other forms of local performance management.

LAAs had an early assessment of their contribution to improved outcomes (DCLG 2006b). This has found that there has already been a distinct influence on shared priorities and the pursuit of shared goals as agencies and individuals begin to work more holistically. Governance is also an issue which is being tackled as local partnership structures are reviewed to make them more fit for a more integrated purpose. However, there is still some way to go, not least in reducing central government performance monitoring requirements at the local level.

Thus, over a 5-year period, a non-statutory approach, LSPs have now moved to a delivery mode. When allied to the review of Devolved Decision Making (HMT 2004a, 2004b, 2006) and the 10-year review of the future of local government, LSPs offer increasingly joined-up public service at the local level.

Conclusions

The development of LSPs offer a glimpse of the future of the local public sector. Although started as 'a good thing' they are developing into a strong force at the local level that is increasingly being reinforced into a new local public service framework. For public bodies outside the local authority, the emerging structure of Local Strategic Partnerships and Local Public Service Boards also bring them back into a democratic framework of local accountability with local authorities in the lead position. The proposals for 'special purpose vehicles' (DCLG 2006) to support delivery will also see a growing organisation with a increasing budget and the ability to employ staff. In time, with appropriate democratic accountability included, this could be the new public service organisation at the local level. Local Government Boards existed before the reform of local government in 1886 to create county and district councils and if the current public service reform trajectory continues we could see a return of the board to run local public services.

The role of the business and voluntary sectors in LSPs remains more problematic. Businesses have low levels of interest in local affairs and although there is some involvement, business interests are frequently represented by government or quasi-government agencies set up to support the local business interests. The voluntary sector can be very disparate at the local level and many local authorities are helping the local voluntary sector to set up umbrella groups. If voluntary and community bodies become more involved in delivering commissioned services or running them directly (as proposed in DCLG 2006) then this relationship may need to alter.

12

PARISHES, TOWN COUNCILS, AND NEIGHBOURHOOD WORKING

all chapter

Introduction

There has been a long-standing debate within the United Kingdom about the issue of local democratic accountability. Although there is a tendency to consider that the United Kingdom is 'overgoverned' with too many tiers of government (an argument which was advanced both in the devolution debates 1997–1999 and in the English regions debate 2000 onwards), each citizen of the United Kingdom has fewer democratic representatives compared with citizens in other countries (Knox 2002). On the other hand, there have been continuing concerns about the number of recently established local bodies which do not have direct accountability to the electorate but rather to their own membership and to their sponsoring government department. However, locally based governance initiatives, or the emergence of 'new localism' or 'glocalism' are seen to be 'desirable' across the world for a number of reasons including

1 wider ownership of decision making;
2 increasing interest in voting thus improving the democratic accountability of decision making;
3 efficiency by reducing layers of bureaucracy;
4 effectiveness in delivery – smaller areas for delivery can provide more targeted approaches.

Since 2001, a national U.K. initiative to generate a more locally based governance approach has been represented in PSA targets – the contracts between government departments and the Treasury, which form the basis of public expenditure. However, much of the debate has been about which local democratic models should be utilised. There are those who through 'new localism' (Corry and Stoker 2002; Balls 2003) argue that the best approach is to enhance the powers of the existing structures of local government and, town and parish councils. The contrary view, which might be called 'central localism' or *new* 'new localism', suggests that local government does not provide the right skills and immediacy for local engagement in local service delivery issues such as those involved in managing the police, health, or education (Blears 2003; Milburn 2003). Miliband (2006a) has termed this as 'double devolution', from the state to local government and from local government to neighbourhoods.

In the local government model, the main argument relates to the principle that only a local authority has an interest across all issues in their locality, whether social, economic, or environmental, and that it is the responsibility of the local authority to deal with them in an accountable way, albeit increasingly with partners. The 'central localism' approach argues that local authorities are synonymous with a lack of local engagement and that Civic renewal would be better generated through areas where people already judge services to be better and there is also evidence of more active engagement at the local level. Detractors of the latter view (Beecham 2005) argue that this creates a new wave of separate organisations while it is also likely that such locally elected police or health boards would retain a Central government focus on delivery without any requirements to join up with other public bodies. This chapter considers these new approaches which are being developed as a means of creating a layer of more local neighbourhood representation in government.

Developments since 1997

As part of the post-1997 approach to community leadership and locally focused working, there have been a number of different initiatives to encourage local governance at a sub-local authority level. These initiatives have built on existing activities but have been enhanced over time. The first was for town and parish councils to further develop their roles and responsibilities. The second was the enhanced role played by neighbourhood renewal and Neighbourhood Development Companies (NDCs), which operate in the most deprived urban and rural areas. Their work is primarily focused on urban areas where deprivation is seen to be most concentrated. The third initiative has emerged from the Local Government Act 2000 following which councils are now able to delegate the responsibility for service delivery to communities or neighbourhoods and give responsibility for this delivery to the councillors and community representatives. This could lead to the creation of local mini-mayors.

Progress on neighbourhood working has been slow to take off in practice in practice and further reforms were proposed in 2006 (DCLG 2006). These included an extension of parishing across all areas in England – urban and rural – and the ability of these parishes to elect to run their own services, including the transfer of assets from local authority to parish level. A new community 'Call for Action' is also proposed as part of this parish package, which is to be exercised by local councillors or through the Overview and Scrutiny Committee.

There are other reasons for promoting a more local, neighbourhood approach, such as the continued concern about political disengagement and lower turnout rates at elections. Studies that have looked at the underlying problems, which cause this lack of engagement, such as that by Whiteley (2002), have shown that Britain is 'civically underdeveloped in many respects' (p. 43), and more individualised. This leads to two further issues – the creation of Putnam's (2000) social capital and the absence of trust. Social capital is seen to be a key component in generating social cohesion, overcoming local tensions, and providing a firm basis for a growing economy. Following Putnam, the Government's Performance and Innovation Unit published a discussion paper *Social Capital* (2002), where these ideas were developed in relation to England. This approach has been of interest in other countries and the OECD, where there has been discussion on the development of a common definition against which countries can measure their social capital performance. In the United Kingdom and Australia, respective statistical agencies have been undertaking projects to use their data to analyse the components of social capital at the local level (Harper 2002). Social capital is seen to be a measure of social cohesion which can only be generated at the local level. The strength of social cohesion is seen to be a function of local activity.

The issue of trust, the second major concern, has also been seen to be a factor in people's failure to engage in the political process. In looking at the issue of trust in public institutions, the Audit Commission and MORI (2003) found that trust is a difficult notion to define, but in situations where citizens use public services, that is, where they have no choice of provider, trust is an important issue for them. In communities, local TV and radio stations were seen to have the greatest 'trust' at 70% in their communications, compared with 22% for local councillors and 11% for national politicians. There was seen to be a declining deference to experts and a strong link between experts and accountability in the public's mind.

Improving trust was seen to be a function of a number of factors, including the provision of more information and the independence of those supplying it. Further, and critically here for the development of neighbourhood policy, trust was seen to be higher in those with whom there was some personal contact – the local decision maker was seen to be more likely to be trusted than someone who was more distant. Thus, 'trust is strengthened by the *visibility* of service delivery' (Audit Commission and MORI, p. 40). The effectiveness of locality based approaches have also been confirmed by other studies such as that by the Audit Commission on *Connecting with Citizens and Users* (2002b), where handing over control to the users was seen to be a key success factor in project and programme delivery.

The contribution of the neighbourhood in generating social capital, trust, and engagement are seen to be important factors in delivering the quality of life and 'liveability' factors, such access to open space, good environmental quality, and access to good public services. Giving the community more control and more choice is seen to be an important factor in the way in which people feel about their community and themselves. The introduction of Anti-social Behaviour Orders

(ASBOs), where communities can deal with 'drug dens' or the 'neighbours from hell' is seen to be an important component for communities exerting control over their own localities. It is at the neighbourhood level that local services which take up the important components of the perceived quality of life are delivered, including health, education, housing, shopping, and public transport (Audit Commission 2002a).

Although these initiatives arise from separate provenances and have differing foci, one of the key issues for the future is how they may be brought together into a more coherent sub-local authority model, which would be similar to the arrangement of local government in other countries such as France. The principle of new localism which provides a legitimising basis for working at the lowest appropriate level – in some ways a re-branded principle of subsidiarity – is now supported not only by political philosophy but also with emerging evidence that smaller government can be both more effective and cost efficient, although only if it is not duplicated at each tier.

Parish and town councils

Although not always considered as a component of neighbourhood governance, Parish Councils have performed this role since at least 1601, if not before and by 2003 there were approximately 8700 local (parish) councils in England. Local councils have a number of powers which they may choose to exercise but very few duties. Ellwood et al. (1992) have identified the main kinds of activities in which local councils have engaged. These have included maintenance of village halls, parks and open spaces, and public toilets. Each parish council has a parish clerk whose task it is to call meetings and ensure that business is run within the legal framework. As such they are similar to local authority chief executives, although on a much smaller scale.

There has been strong encouragement for the development of 'local councils', which can have a range of functions and roles. The ability of local councils to take on new roles was enhanced by the Local Government and Rating Act 1997, when it became possible for local councils to undertake the provision of additional services including public transport, traffic calming, and community safety. The extension of the role of local councils was proposed through the creation of Quality Parish and Town Councils (2001, 2003) which allowed those local councils wanting to be designated as 'quality' councils to have enhanced roles such as consultation, provision of services, and information. This approach has also been accompanied by new powers provided for local councils to increase the level of funding which is to be utilised to £5 per head. This can be used on projects that bring direct benefit to there area but for which there may not otherwise be the powers. This funding is authorised within the power of s. 137 of the Local Government Act 1972. There is also an intention that central government should be able to fund local councils directly in future, although this will need new legislation.

The 1997 Act also made it possible for residents to petition for the establishment of a parish council in their area and over 107 new parish councils have been created (Bevan 2003). The reasons for forming a new parish council reflect those of much of the community and neighbourhood management movement – a sense of frustration in the way in which a particular locality is dealt with by the local authority and other agencies (Bevan 2003). The selection of the parish council to take more local control of matters is based on assumptions that this model has both a permanent and an independent status than other forms of neighbourhood partnership. Parish councils are also seen to have more generic structures which would enable them to take on different issues simultaneously or over time. The parish council, which is set up on an open electoral basis, is also seen to be potentially more accountable and capable of holding a variety of interests rather than a more tightly focused single-issue group The parish council model is appropriate to any locality wanting to engage in neighbourhood management and can sit alongside other forms of locality management such as local authorities or their neighbourhood management arrangements.

One long-standing concern has been the lack of a code of conduct for members of parish councils. Since 2000, those elected to local authorities have been required to register their personal interests in a public register and to declare them publicly if a relevant matter is to come before the council. In some cases, councillors have to withdraw from meetings and not take part in any discussion or decision making about specific issues in which they are deemed to have an interest. Until the introduction of the Local Government Act 2000, these provisions did not apply to parish councils, but each parish council has now to adopt a local code of conduct. The Parish Councils (Model Code of Conduct) Order 2001 was introduced and any complaints against violations of the code are dealt with by the local authority within which the parish council sits. The adoption of this code has led to a considerable debate amongst parish councillors and, in some cases, large numbers of councillors have resigned from their seats because they have been unwilling to declare their financial interests.

Although town and parish councils vary in the way in which they operate at the local level, with some being far more active than others, there are a number of key issues which relate to all democratically elected governance bodies. The first is that it is often both difficult to encourage residents to stand as parish or town councillors and there is always local pressure to avoid holding elections, which have to be funded directly by the parish council. Hence there are concerns about the democratic mandate of the local councils. A further issue is how far parish councillors represent the interests of their locality. The introduction of the code of conduct has been a means of identifying the interests of individual parish councillors particularly when commenting on land, planning, and development issues that often give the greatest cause for local concern.

A second set of issues extend to the way in which parish and town councils relate both to other community organisations in the same locality and to the local authorities which cover the broader areas within which they sit. Bevan (2003) shows that these relationships may lack considerable trust and can be conflictual. Often a community group or a new town council may be established in order to make progress on issues which are seen not to be sufficiently high priority for the upper tier council. As Bevan (2003) shows, new councils can be seen as a threat to existing groups, which may already have a role in representing the community on existing overarching partnerships such as the LSP.

Devolved working in local authorities

The introduction of new council constitutions in the Local Government Act 2000 provided the opportunity for local authorities to operate some services and decision making at sub-authority level through some form of area-based committees. These provisions were intended both to develop the opportunity for a more local input into decision making over issues which are of direct relevance and to provide a greater role for ward councillors. Leach et al. (2003) report that over half of local authorities in England have some form of area-based working. The two main forms are area forums and area committees, with the former being generally consultative. Area committees can have decision-making powers devolved to them. In the Leach et al. (2003) study, a number of specific authorities are quoted where these experiments are taking place including Warwickshire, Barnsley, Tameside, and Oxford. The arrangements for area-based working vary according to each council. In some, specific, albeit small, budgets have been allocated to enable work to be undertaken, with local decision making on specific priorities.

Leach et al. (2003) identified some lessons for councils wishing to develop effective area arrangements:

1   The design of area based arrangements needs to be seen in the context of the council's overall approach to enhancing local democracy. It is better to take small steps that are successful and can be sustained than to start a major decentralisation process that has a high risk of becoming disconnected from the council's mainstream activities.
2   Ward and divisional councillors should be supported in their 'area' role through the provision of appropriate and accessible information on their 'patch', including regular updates on the plans and activities of the council and other agencies.
3   Area forums and committees need to engage all relevant stakeholders in order to enable an effective response to community agendas that cut across organisational boundaries.
4   Members and officers with an area role need to be able to contribute their perspective in council-wide or functional areas – without this, the area dimension will not be able to realise its full potential.

Val's comment

5 The availability of budgets at an area level increases the profile and impact of area arrangements. These budgets may be the council's but may also derive from those other agencies working on an area basis – e.g. health or regeneration partnerships.
6 Holding meetings in accessible venues at appropriate times and on matters of local interest are key ways to engage the public. (Leach et al. 2003, p. 47)

Emerging forms of local management

There are numerous other examples of area-based management approaches which have been implemented in an attempt to overcome local problems or tensions. Knox et al. (2002) describe some specific approaches for mixed tenure neighbourhoods, which is a particularly important issue in housing estates where part of the stock has been sold while the rest remains under local authority management. Such management approaches need to have a strong involvement and representation from residents from an early stage to be successful although it is still possible for residents to feel 'alienated' from those active in neighbourhood management. Knox et al. (2002) also compare these more active neighbourhood management approaches with other forms of local governance including the management company approach and that offered by a parish council, for example. For housing purposes, they concluded that a firmer legal vehicle would be the most effective route because it seeks not only to facilitate residents' participation in local governance but also recognises the need for wider stakeholder involvement.

The development of partnership working at sub-authority level has been in a number of other ways. One is the BID approach, based on the U.S. model, which seeks to provide additional benefits to businesses which are funded from the businesses directly through their own local contributions. These BIDs are seen to be central to both local regeneration and to the United Kingdom's competitiveness. The implementation of BIDs was included in the Local Government Act 2003. BIDs are defined as 'partnership arrangements through which local authorities and local businesses can take forward schemes which benefit the whole community subject to the agreement of the ratepayers' (ODPM 2003b, p. 6). In this case, the 'ratepayers' are those located within any BID and their agreement is critical because they will be required to pay an additional levy to fund the work in their area. Within the scheme the funding is held in the BID account, which has to be set up by the relevant local authority participating in the scheme and it is also possible for those within the bid to make additional contributions to those raised by the levy.

BIDs can be in any area and are envisaged to be able to encompass a wide range of projects which will help to promote the BID's core activities such as increasing footfall (as a measure of potential sales) in a retail centre or improving security in an industrial estate. Individual projects can vary in scale and type, within their partnership programme, including CCTV, physical improvement, and training measures. BIDs can also span two local authority areas, with one local authority being responsible for their administration. There is some involvement from the voluntary sector and organisations such as Groundwork, which undertake specific improvement tasks, as well as being linked with existing projects funded by the government, EU, lottery, or other funding programmes. The local community should be involved in the BID. One of the first BIDs is in the city of Westminster in the Leicester Square/Piccadilly Circus area.

As with other partnerships, there will be concerns about the nature of account-ability. The BID Board is derived from the local stakeholders but which 'must also comprise individuals with the requisite skills to put together a successful BID proposal (ODPM 2003b, p. 20). BIDs can only be established after a formal vote and as such may be similar to a more local version of a parish or town council with the ability to raise a precept. BIDs can also only have a life of 5 years before their mandate needs to be renewed through fresh elections.

Neighbourhood development in the future

The drive to promote neighbourhood renewal is also coming from the centre, where different government departments have been given PSA targets in order to help tackle social exclusion. In the 2004 Comprehensive Spending Review, these targets cover decent homes, economic performance, liveability, road safety, life expectancy, health inequalities, children's development, and crime reduction. In addition to these targets being included within each department's agreement for delivery, these are also included within each department's cross-sectoral five-year plans which were published early in 2005 (e.g. ODPM 2005b). In this, the overarching objectives for neighbourhoods are shown as follows:

Our aim is to create *sustainable communities* – places that offer people

1   A decent home that they can afford.
2   A community in which they want to live and work.
3   The chance to develop their skills and interests.
4   Access to jobs and excellent services.
5   The chance to get engaged in their community and to make a difference. (ODPM 2005b, para. 1.2, p. 6)

Much of this approach confirms the role of the neighbourhood in achieving these broader objectives in all localities, including those not needing specific support for regeneration. This approach which is also being mirrored across Europe through its territorial cohesion policy (CEC 2007). The more detailed proposals for engaging citizens in the management of their communities in England are set out in *Why Neighbourhoods Matter* (ODPM 2005c), which is also a daughter document of the Ten Year Review of local government (ODPM 2004l). In this, there is a strong association between the level of electoral turnout and the extent to which local issues are discussed during elections – at whatever scale.

There is also a recognition that people want to 'influence decisions in the public services to meet their needs' (ODPM 2004l, p. 8). The framework for neighbourhood governance is expected to take into account five key principles:

1   All councils, in partnership with other providers, should provide opportunities and support for neighbourhood engagement through appropriate arrangements so that they can respond to the needs and priorities of neighbourhood communities;
2   neighbourhood arrangements must be capable of making a real difference to the everyday lives of citizens;
3   the nature of neighbourhood arrangements must be appropriate to local circumstances, be flexible to changing circumstances over time and be responsive to the needs and diversity of the community and its organisations;
4   neighbourhood arrangements must be consistent with local representative democracy which gives legitimacy to governmental institutions, and places elected councillors as the leading advocates for their communities and with the requirements of local democratic accountability;
5   neighbourhood arrangements must be balanced with the demands of efficiency and proportionality. (ODPM 2005c, p. 12)

The role of the neighbourhood using these frameworks to establish new governance approaches, includes managing the establishment of local priorities, setting performance standards, managing some budgets, and, in some cases, having responsibility for delivering services. In all these approaches there is a strong expectation of community engagement within a democratic framework.

For councillors, the emerging neighbourhood framework creates a new role in their wards and communities which may address the perceived lack of connectivity for the majority of local authority councillors with council agenda setting since the introduction of the new local authority constitutional arrangements in 2000. Like parish councils, neighbourhood bodies will be covered by a code of conduct in order to provide reassurance about the openness of decision taking. This move to greater neighbourhood devolution has been supported by another initiative for *Vibrant Local Leadership* (ODPM 2005d), which is primarily targeted at local councillors and the political leadership. It remains to be seen whether local councillors use the community 'Call for Action' at local level or whether parish will take on local authority assets and services in a more routine way. 'Neighbourhoodisation' seems to be the reverse of more efficient working which consistently highlights the benefits of larger scale working. There are ways that they can both work together but no clear lead on ways to assess their relative merits in delivery.

Conclusions

There is no doubt that the development of the role of the neighbourhood governance body in the management of communities and localities is emerging as one of the most significant in the next 10 years. In the period before 1997, local authorities were concerned about their own role and rights for independence. Many of the reforms in the period since 1997 have been aimed at helping to achieve this, although local authorities may argue that greater local authority independence from targets is still required. The period from 2005 to 2010 and possibly longer to 2025 is one where the role of the neighbourhood in establishing social cohesion, along the lines suggested by Putnam (2000) and increasing greater democratic engagement, is on the agenda.

This approach is also part of a higher level political philosophy which is part of the move towards achieving *choice* in public services and more *contestability* for the user in terms of the provider, whether this be health, education, or care (Lent and Arend 2004). Milburn (2005) identifies four key components in this process, which he has based on his own experience of public services while growing up in the North East. These are

1   better information, greater choice;
2   strengthening citizens' voice;
3   shifting accountability outwards and onwards;
4   devolving power to local neighbourhoods. (Milburn 2005, p. 30)

Much of this imposed delegation may be controversial to local authorities, who may see their newly achieved status and role being undermined. Milburn confirms the need for neighbourhood bodies to be accountable, although it is not clear to whom they should be accountable – the local authority, a regional body, or government departments. Some local authorities are very critical about the promotion of a new tier of governance in areas where communities are already confused about who represents them and who is accountable for service delivery.

The reforms at neighbourhood level are significant while many of the potential problems and issues are yet to be fully examined. They also sit within a reformed local governance structure which is generated by LAAs, where the local public services can be seen to be merging together in common public sector programmes or though Local Public Service Boards. As the local authority becomes more managerial and programme orientated, led by its executive or directly elected mayor, the neighbourhood could be the level at which proposals are developed to meet problems, where solutions are delivered, and where people and communities make choices over their priorities and provider in the application of the choice principle.

What is less clear is how local decision making sits within national targetry. Local authorities have frequently complained that local partnerships, including LSPs, cannot tackle local priorities within a framework of nationally set targets for bodies such as the police and health. If this system remains, the complexity of local delivery may be considerable. All main political parties are committed to greater local devolution and this means that there will need to be a new breed of local political leaders and managers in order to implement this emerging and seemingly increasingly important tier of neighbourhood governance.

13

REGIONS, SUB-REGIONS, AND LONDON

Introduction

Regional policy has been active in the United Kingdom since its introduction in the 1930s, as a response to economic decline, and during this long period it has had many forms. Until 1973, regional policy was a domestic matter, set by government and managed through a variety of schemes including the establishment of new towns. In 1973, U.K. regional policy became a matter to be determined by the EU, although in 2003, the Chancellor of the Exchequer sought to have regional policy returned to member states under the subsidiarity principle (HMT 2004b). The devolution of power to Scotland, Wales, and Northern Ireland, after 1997, has left England in an anomalous position. England neither has power devolved to the state as a whole (and if so, who represents the government of England?) nor does it have power devolved to its regions, following the failed attempt to create democratically elected regional assemblies in 2004.

Nevertheless, the issue of the governance of England is coming to the fore, not least as Wales now has agreement to pursue a similar set of powers as have been given to Scotland (Richard 2004). Lyons has started to make a contribution to this debate (Lyons 2006) and has identified a new approach to central and local government working in England. He has proposed that there should be more clarity about who is responsible for what in local and central government and to implement local devolution:

> By devolution, I therefore mean that we need to shift the balance of responsibilities for public services from central to local government, and to be clearer about their respective roles and responsibilities. (Lyons 2006, para. 4.6)

At the same time as regional policy has been developing there have also been other changes in the hierarchy of spatial governance in England. In 2004, *The Northern Way* (www.thenorthernway.org.uk) was launched. This is an economic strategy for a combination of three English regions – the North East, the North West, and Yorkshire and Humberside, and subsequently followed by the Midlands Way. This is being followed by a similar approach in the East and West Midlands. Below regional level, there has been a significant development in the establishment of sub-regions, which may be based on administrative or 'natural' areas (www.english-nature.org.uk). Both meta-regions and sub-regions represent interesting developments, not least as they do not have traditional governance or political representation structures. Any arrangements for working together at these scales are local and cooperative. They need new forms of working in order to succeed and there are other parallels. The meta-regions begin to look similar in size to Scotland, Wales, and Northern Ireland although there are no proposals to establish devolved governance arrangements at these scales in England.

For the sub-regions, their role could be to generate constituencies in any future form of regional accountable democratic structure. They also provide a contextual framework for city regions as the proposals to create city development companies and MAAs suggest (DCLG 2006c). City regions in this format are primarily focused on the economic role of cities in helping to promote national economic prosperity. Their boundaries are defined by their 'economic footprint' – possibly the area covered by the average journey to work time of 45 min into the city centre. These city regions will have a unified approach to planning, transport, housing, and economic investment and have this as their main focus. However, the social and environmental infrastructure could follow this lead in due course.

One of the further concerns about the current arrangements for working at sub-national level is the plethora of schemes and funds which may often have competing and conflicting objectives even where they are designed to support the same areas or the same communities. It is this fragmentation which is seen to undermine the support given, reduce its impact, and increase its operational costs. Perri 6 et al. (2002) also define fragmentation as implying a transfer of costs from one provider to another. In a review of ABIs undertaken by the government's English Regional Coordination Unit (ODPM/RCU 2002), a commitment was made to tackle this issue through the reduction in the variety of funding streams. A report of progress made in June 2003 seems to demonstrate that very few practical steps have been taken apart from some commitment to mainstreaming (ODPM 2003f). Since this, the announcement of the establishment of LAAs in July 2004 (ODPM 2004k) has created a local means of bringing together funding schemes and agencies.

There is also a move to bring together the ways in which the initiatives at various spatial scales will work together in an approach, which will need a considerable degree of coordination in a much looser government structure. The role of spatial planning, for example, in delivering these inter-connected programmes for delivery could increase in importance following the adoption of the provisions in the 2004 Planning and Compensation Act.

Although elected regional assemblies may be delayed indefinitely, there is pressure to move to greater autonomy for the regions in a variety of issues particularly for economic development and regeneration. This is likely to bring an increase in the local management of funding which has been managed by central government hitherto (HMT 2007). This is practical regionalism that is promoting more regional working but without the democratic framework and leadership that might have gone with it within a directly elected regional assembly. There are also proposals to move government functions to the regions and away from Whitehall (Lyons 2004), similar to the practices of regional dispersal and decision making in other EU member states such as Italy and Ireland. The regional tier seems set to grow in importance, and while the destination seems clear, the routes are yet to be finally determined.

Why regionalism?

Since 1973, there has been a re-focusing on the role of regions in their own right. As Keating et al. (2003, p. 6) state, 'For over one hundred years, the context for regional politics and policies have been the nation-state, with regions being the object rather than the subject of policy'. As Keating et al. go on to argue, some assumptions about the growth of globalisation has led to the view that the link between territory and economic performance is now lost, but there is also a counter trend, which suggests that economic performance is driven from the local rather than the central (HMT 2004b). Within the EU, the structural funds have been used to bring together regions which have common interests to develop their solidarity and to share lessons. These links have been created in two ways. First, in areas which are geographical neighbours such as in the European mega regions generated from Europe 2000 + (CEC 2002). The second approach has been to encourage the grouping of regions around common interests such as telecities or coalfield communities.

How successful have these initiatives been in generating both economic improvement and more cultural identity, both of which lead to more solidarity? Fothergill (1994) argues that groups of areas are more likely to be taken seriously in discussions with the EU than individual local authorities. Such alliances can face considerable challenges of distance, language, competition for investment, and no existing means of working together. Fothergill examines one grouping, that of coal field regions within the EU, where although these disadvantages prevailed, as mining is an industry which has real dangers associated with its practices greater collectivist and community-based legacy than other industries which has supported mutual interest. Based on the influence which the coalfield regions group EUR-ACOM had in the European Commission, Fothergill (1994) concludes that it is possible to have this influence at the local and regional level without requiring the support of central government.

The ability of regions to work together without the support of central government has been one of the factors in encouraging greater devolution and regional governance within the United Kingdom. Other main drivers for regionalism in England have been recognised such as environmental sustainability (Slater 2003). The potential for producing fresh produce within a region can enhance the quality of the food and reduce transport costs for the producer and consumer. There are also benefits in developing regional food specialities for added-value production and supporting pride in regional excellence. There are also potential benefits for intra-regional distribution of growth and development where this is an issue. Regions could also foster a more polycentric approach to their development, as different places make a different contribution within the region.

The role of the regions in generating the national economy has also come to the fore since 2003. The Core Cities Group (ODPM 2004a) is generating a new approach to national economic growth. Some of the more traditional approaches of strategic intervention in sectors or localities are giving way to an approach which sees local innovation and small- and medium-sized company growth as key determinants of national GDP. Conversely, as *Frontier Economics* found in a report commissioned by the ODPM, HMT, and DTI in 2004, 'there is a developing evidence base, in areas of education and skills, employment and enterprise, that indicates the critical role played by place based factors such as peer effects, neighbourhood and intergenerational effects' (p. 1).

Regional working in England 1993–2004 – moving from central ways of working

The establishment of GOs for the regions in 1993 seemed to be an unexpected move on the part of a government which had not necessarily been supportive of the decentralisation of decision making or of sub-national policy interventions in the economy. The GOs were an amalgamation of the regional functions of a number of government departments including the then Department of the Environment (which included planning, local government, and housing) and the Department of Transport. Other departments frequently had observers or those responsible for some functions sitting within the GOs such as the Home Office on crime reduction issues and the Department for Environment, Food and Rural Affairs (DEFRA) for rural policy. The relationship between these different government department representatives was described as one of 'co-location', with the regional director having responsibility for the GO and all its work, but individual members of staff in the GOs having a dual reporting line to their 'home' departments. During the period 1994–1999, the GOs were seen to be primarily offices where all civil servants with an interest in the region sat together but conducted their business separately.

The approach to GOs was changed within the second period of their operation, 1999–2004. The first change was in the appointment of regional directors from a wider pool of candidates rather than career civil servants. Former local authority chief executives became regional directors of GOs in some regions, for example, the West Midlands, East Midlands, and South East. Within the GOs other changes started to appear. First, there was a move to area-based working rather than organising by departmental functions. This responsibility for part of the region was combined with a lead for rural policy or local government practice in a matrix management structure. This also led to the establishment of the emergent sub-regional structures for management of issues within regions. During this period a wider of range of government departments also started to join the GOs.

The proposals for directly elected regional assemblies in some regions, as contained in the regional white paper *Your Region Your Choice* in ODPM 2003h caused some initial debate about the role of the GOs in these regions. There were also other concerns about the arrangements in the regions where no directly elected regional assembly was proposed. On the second point, the regional white paper included integrating proposals for regional working within government, commonly known as the 'chapter 2' approach, which all GOs have been moving towards. These now form the basis of the relationship in all regions. The gradual move towards more integrated working at regional level was enhanced in 2003 with the appointment of directors of Local Government Practice in each GO, again appointed from those with direct local government experience. This role was established to take responsibility for the local government improvement agenda in an integrated way and the new role for GOs in the negotiation of LAAs from 2004.

During this period of the establishment and growth of GOs, Regional Development Agencies (RDAs) were also established to bring together a more combined and programmed approach to the delivery of funding available for the region from the EU and central government resources. Like the GOs, the RDAs did not have any democratic structure underpinning them although each RDA had a board comprised of local business and educational interests together with some local political representation. The RDAs each have a chief executive and like the GOs these posts have been widened to attract former local government chief executives. The RDAs have been seen to be proactive in their approaches to improving regional GDP and GVA and their contribution to the economy of the country as a whole (HMT 2004b).

The extent to which these two key regional structures work together must depend on local personalities and a common agenda, and there was some expectation that under a directly elected regional assembly model the RDAs would be placed more centrally under a democratically accountable mandate.

At the same time as these government initiatives have been developing, each English region has also established its own indirectly elected regional assembly comprising of local politicians and representatives of community, voluntary, and business bodies. These regional assemblies have operated differently with the East Midlands being seen as the most successful as working with GOEM and the RDA in combining a regional economic and spatial strategy. Within regions the policy direction has been one which has gradually been moving away from that which is focused on particular localities or groups of people within the region to a more combined approach of both funding and alignment of aims within the regional level. This is supported by a more joined-up approach at the local level as expressed through LAAs negotiated by the GOs. England is now in a position which makes it possible to deliver a more combined approach to area-based funding as set out in the EU's Territorial Cohesion policies (CEC 2007) which will run from 2007 to 2013. These policies are more interested in whole place strategies and the ways in which they work together.

Regionalising the centre

The dominance of Whitehall and Westminster in policy development and influence has been as a long-term issue. Devolution in Scotland, Wales, and Northern Ireland has 'repatriated' policy making to those devolved governments but this challenge remains alive in England, where there is still an operational confusion in the governance between policy development for the nation and policy development for England. The arrangements for devolved governance mean that all parts of the United Kingdom do not implement the same policies in the same way at the same time. Inevitably this approach is tempered by politics – any government can operate its political organisation cooperatively to achieve some common outcomes which will also be informed by experience in different territories. There are also external factors which drive similarities in policy not least deriving from the implementation of EU legislation and initiatives and beyond this there are the pressures from the WTO.

Critics of the Londonisation of policy have been active for some years. The arguments are summarised by Amin et al. (2003, p. 2) in a debate over the 'geography of British Power'. For such an approach to work 'requires more than a simple devolution of powers, but a radically new way of imagining spatiality of the nation too: no longer the norm of a centred nation with tributary obligations, but the promise of a multi-nodal nation' (Amin et al. 2003, p. 3). In order to progress this, Amin et al. suggest moving the national capital out of London to different parts of the country in turn although they acknowledge that 'Whitehall' in the regions is a more likely prospect.

How have these regional arrangements worked for local government in England?

The relationships between individual local authorities and their GOs and RDAs vary with some finding them to be more useful than others. Research by the LGA

(2003a) demonstrated that local authorities were reporting positive relationships, with their GOs (78%), their RDAs (64%), and their regional assembles (43%). The same range of relationships is found with a variety of other agencies operating within the region, with the poorest relationship being recorded with the Strategic Rail Authority (17%) (2003). However, local authorities viewed the implementation of directly elected regional government with some concern. The LGA (2003a) study demonstrated that the main issues were subsidiarity, transparency, and accountability. There was also an underlying concern about the loss of functions from local to regional level. The position seemed to differ from that in Scotland, Wales, and Northern Ireland where it was expected that the relationship would improve. The expectation for English local authorities was similar to that found in London.

Sub-regions

The concept of formal sub-regional working surfaced first in the Senior Minority Report to the Redcliffe–Maud Report of the Royal Commission on Local Government in England 1966–1969 (Cmnd 4040). Senior, a member of the Commission, published a Memorandum of Dissent to the report that advocated the establishment of 35 city-region governance arrangements. Some local authorities now believe that the failure to pursue this approach is leading to a lack of competitiveness in England compared with other parts of Europe and the United States (Birmingham 2003) and are seeking to address the issue. This concern for the competitiveness of sub-regions, in this case particularly city-regions, has been considered by a government working party which includes the Core Cities Group and RDAs. In their second report (ODPM et al. 2003), the key driver for active sub-regional working is seen to be European competitiveness together with the disparities in performance and productivity within English sub-regions. Evidence also demonstrates that national and regional economic performance is dependent on the performance of major cities in the knowledge-based industries. Cities are seen to be the 'powerhouse' of modern economies (ODPM et al. 2003, p. 5). However, this report also stresses the importance of the relationship between city-regions and the rest of their regions. Although acting as economic drivers, they depend on the rest of the region for their labour force, markets, and capacity for further growth as well as providing the cultural and environmental space for the region to offer a balanced life style to its citizens (ODPM, HMT, and DTI, June 2003).

The emergence of sub-regional working as a growing practice since 1996 has been encouraged but has not yet evolved as a common framework. Each region has developed its own approach, generally through sub-regional partnerships with the East Midlands taking the most proactive lead. Elsewhere, each of the GOs has established sub-regional teams. The main drivers for working in sub-regions for local authorities have been varied, ranging from the need to promote their voice in a region which is normally weighted towards other influences, to those where improved working can lead to both greater citizen benefits and organisational efficiency through service delivery and procurement. In some cases, councils which have been classified as weak or failing in the CPA process have been encouraged to work with neighbouring councils which have had a stronger performance evaluation. Some sub-regions have been established across estuaries or rivers such as Thames Gateway, Newcastle Gateshead, Hull, and North Lincs. Finally, some sub-regions have started to work together in response to funding often generated from the EU for urban or rural regeneration (e.g. the Lea Valley, the Black Country).

Sub-regions are characterised by being polycentric, thus making them different from a conurbation model, where a major city will act as a hub to draw in population for work, public functions, and culture. The model of sub-regions as polycentric areas, with complementary provision of services and facilities is based on the experience in Germany where, apart from Berlin, no individual city dominates its hinterland in the same way as the major British cities. Sub-regional approaches are also being used as new policy tools to deal with areas of new growth such as that around Milton Keynes or areas of housing market renewal in Lancashire, where the housing market is seen not to be supporting regeneration. In both these examples, the sub-regions are clustered across administrative and sometimes regional borders such as the approach in the Thames Gateway. Sub-regional identification has also been seen to be important for social cohesion, identity, and community solidarity. The recognition of the sub-regional role for cultural, economic, and sustainable purposes represents a major shift in policy practice in England.

The nature of sub-regional working varies in delivery. In the Black Country, a wide range of partners within the Black Country Consortium has produced a vision for the future, *Looking Forward: The Black Country in 2033* (2003). This vision is expected to be the starting point for the development of a comprehensive plan which is expected to overcome many of the challenges which the sub-region faces. The city-region approach has been adopted by Birmingham, which has produced a prospectus for 'enhancing the competitiveness and renaissance of the Birmingham city-region (2003). This city-region includes nine local authorities including those which comprise the Black Country consortium, demonstrating that sub-regional arrangements can be overlapping – at present there is no sense in which of these arrangements have to be one per local authority. Local authorities are joining sub-regional partnerships to cover as many of their specific interests as they consider appropriate. The Birmingham city-region is 'led' by Birmingham, rather than being seen as a partnership thus illustrating a further difference between conurbation and polycentric approaches to sub-regional action although both types of sub-regional consortia seek to have a 'special relationship' with central government in meeting their own particular agendas, which includes 'distinctiveness'. There are other examples of sub-regional partnerships such as the Welland.

Some sub-regions cross two or more regions such as the Oxford to Cambridge Arc – O2C Arc – which not only crosses the SE and the eastern region but also includes the East Midlands. O2C Arc is a knowledge-based sub-region, which has generally poor internal communications but shares many of the same interests and challenges. In England it is one of the main drivers of the economy, after London, and is set to grow in importance. The O2C Arc has stated its approach in *The Spirit of Innovation* (2003), which concentrates on the contribution which the sub-region makes to innovation, from academic and business organisations. Unlike some of the other sub-regions, O2C Arc comprises of a partnership of a range of bodies and led by the private sector. The arc's action plan concentrates on issues of infrastructure and technology transfer to ensure that the innovation generated is put into commercial effect. Within this sub-region, there are also attempts to develop competitiveness and enterprise such as the Enterprising Oxford Group (Chadwick et al. 2003; Lawton Smith et al. 2003), which has considered both the conditions which have led to a high-tech cluster within and around the city of Oxford understanding how further innovation and enterprise can be encouraged.

Within each sub-region there is characteristically an increasingly joined-up approach between all the agencies involved. In part, this is not only driven by competition providing a wider context for effort at the local level but it is also seen to contribute to the economic competitiveness of the country as a whole (ODPM et al. 2003). It differs in many ways from earlier approaches to economic planning in a more 'bottom-up' approach.

Although set within a national framework, the characteristic of all these sub-regional approaches is the utilisation of local strengths and weaknesses. Although some sub-regions may not have been seen as major contributors to the regional economy in the past, the new approach suggests that every part of England has a contribution to make. This mirrors the emerging European approach which is also moving away from concentrating on areas of economic decline to one which is wholly inclusive but locally focused.

Sub-regions are emerging as a critical level of local policy development and delivery, and this has been confirmed in the *Sub-national Review of Economic Development and Regeneration* (HMT 2007). In this, governance arrangements across sub-regions are seen to be voluntary and can evolve into new authorities if the constituent authorities of these new sub-regions agree. This could have the longer term effect of restructuring the whole of English sub-national governance arrangements and complete the unfinished work of local government reorganisation, to create unitary rather than two-tier local government. The progress of sub-regions has been advanced by their recognition as programme delivery areas by RDAs in their regional economic strategies processes. As Liddle and Townsend (2003) demonstrate, in the North East, One North East (the RDA) has devolved 75% of its budget to four sub-regional partnerships, each of which has measurable objectives. This process is expected to be enhanced through total devolution of funding to sub-regions once they are established.

London

The legacy of London government following the abolition of the GLC in 1987 had been a major item on the political agenda in 1997. There was an expectation that the government would in some way reverse what was seen as one of the most political acts undertaken by Mrs Thatcher, the abolition of the GLC. It had both symbolic and practical consequences. At a symbolic level, the removal of London government was seen as a price that was being paid for the active development of political voice at a sub-national level. There were also wider implications for the relationship between the central state and the rest of the country. If London, one of the world's largest and most important cities, did not have its own governance structures, this was an outward sign of the movement to state centralism. The ability of to take a strategic action without any specific governance layer was also seen to be problematic. It would always be difficult for 33 strong boroughs with their own political leadership to promote London on the world stage with a single voice. This was also seen to be an issue when London wished to promote its case to government and externally on as in the capture of major sporting events such as the Olympics. The co-ordinating role within London for the period from 1987 was held by the London office of the DoE and then subsequently the GO for London following its establishment in 1994.

The changes in London's governance following the 1997 election exhibited a shift away from viewing London as a political problem to a realisation that London was critical to the United Kingdom's economy and that the complexity of its governance was hampering progress (Walker 2004a). Since London governance has been changed in fundamental ways at regular periods since 1837 (Travers 2004), and the arrangements implemented in 2000 following the 1999 London Mayoral Referendum is another stage in this history. The mayor and the Greater London Authority (GLA), elected directly to 14 geographically based seats and by proportional representation for 11 London wide seats, remained different from any other part of the United Kingdom (Corry 2004a) until the local government elections in Scotland in 2007. The mayor has responsibility for four executive bodies – the police, fire and rescue, transport, and regeneration through the London Development Agency with all four being held to account through the GLA.

The members of the GLA have three powers – the budget, staffing, and general scrutiny. The way in which each of these powers has been exercised has varied. For the budget, it is the whole budget which has to be challenged at the time it is set. To overturn the budget it needs a two-thirds majority of the assembly. While there has been a public debate on priorities, it is also argued that the work between the main political parties behind the scenes has had a significant effect on the budget size and composition each year (Biggs 2004). The use of the assembly's powers in scrutiny and staff appointments is seen to be less successful (Corry et al. 2004). Others argue that the assembly has been 'weak and ineffective'

(Buck et al. 2002, p. 347) with the real checks and balances to the mayor's powers coming from the boroughs rather than the GLA. Although the relationship between the mayor and the assembly will mature and develop, Biggs (2004) argues that the assembly should have more of a sense of its own purpose and unity for London.

There were also concerns about the economic performance of London as a result of its lack of unifying governance or a single voice. Evidence shows that economic performance of London started to rise in the same year as the GLC was dismantled. This is likely to be a historical coincidence rather than a necessary cause (Travers 2004). At the same time research on core cities and competition (ODPM/HMT and DTI 2003) has demonstrated that coherence on the part of major cities is critical to the economic growth of the country as a whole.

Through the period of this first term of the GLA, a different kind of government has been developing in London in comparison with elsewhere in the country. These are differences in the powers, scale, and scope of the operation of the new London governance arrangements. The mayor has responsibility for the London Development Agency whereas elsewhere in England the Secretary of State retains the power of appointment of the RDAs. The police authority reports to the mayor, but the chief constable of the Metropolitan Police Force is regarded as the lead police officer in the country and is appointed by the Home Secretary. This creates tensions in supporting policing for London. Like other directly elected mayors, the mayor of London has the power of appointment over the office holders for these agency posts but not for his chief executive, which is subject to agreement by the GLA. The GLA members can be selected to perform specific roles by the mayor including chairing the police authority and Transport for London (TfL) while other members of the GLA have a scrutiny function. Finally, the GLA is elected on a mixed electoral method which includes both direct candidate election and PR, similar to the Scottish Parliament.

The work of the first few years of mayoral government in London resulted in the adoption of some innovative policies such as the introduction of congestion charging, while some policy processes such as the Spatial Plan for London have also been undertaken much more quickly than was the case in the past. At the same time, the mayor has developed a working relationship with the Association of London Government and the Government of Office for London, which had its powers substantially reduced at the time the new mayoral system was introduced.

In 2006, new powers for the mayor were proposed to cover:

- housing
- skills
- waste
- planning
- culture
- sport
- health

- climate change
- appointments to functional bodies.

At the same time, it was also proposed that the GLA would receive greater scrutiny powers. These additional powers considerably strengthen the role of the mayor and the strategic leadership that the mayor's role can provide. In time these powers may also be available to leaders or mayors of the new city regions.

The government of London is still viewed as a work in progress. The boroughs see the mayor's position as contestable in some areas including his major policy leads and this relationship will mature over time. The GLA is legally described as local authority and is subject to all the local authority processes including BV and CPA although it is viewed as a regional body in practice. With the development of city regions at sub-regional level, across England their governance arrangements may be more like London in due course.

Assessments of the effectiveness of the new arrangements in London are now being considered. Although Sandford (2004a) has defined some weaknesses including a lack of executive power and the scale of the task in terms of the preparation of the 10 key strategies, he also identified ways in which the mayor has been successful. The first is that the mayor has been able to take a lead on issues which have no other obvious institutional home, citing the London Health Commission or new areas of public policy such as the London Hydrogen Alliance which has been created to share national air quality objectives. The second success, which both Sandford (2004b) and Jenkins (2004) identify is in the field of planning and transport, where there have been strategic gains in terms of the preparation of the Spatial Strategy and practical benefits in the increased utilisation of buses and congestion charging. However, Sandford's overall conclusion is that the mayor's ability to have a strong leadership role is ultimately hampered by a lack of direct powers.

From the view of the local authorities in London, the role of the mayor and its relative success brings forward different views. The LGA which represents all local authorities in the country takes the view that the experience of local authorities of implementing devolved government in London is not seen to be so successful as the reforms in Scotland and Wales (LGA 2003b). The prime weakness identified is the inability to generate a common and unified vision. Further, the 'framework and nature of the GLA does not engender the same ownership and pride as a national assembly' (LGA 2003b, p. 8). London governance is seen to be more diffuse than elsewhere with many bodies required to have relationships with central government, GOs, and the mayor. For London boroughs, this was always likely to be a difficult relationship with some boroughs opposed to the establishment of a London-wide governance structure from the outset, although there seems to be some evidence of closer inter-borough working since the GLA was established (Corry 2004a). At the point when London governance arrangements were changed in 1985, the main preoccupation could have been seen to be the vertical links between the GLC and the London boroughs. However as Slaughter (2004) points out, there is a different set of relationships, with other local public agency partners, which are now at least as important as those with a more strategic body. An individual borough may see these vertical and horizontal relationships as being important but not mutually exclusive (LBHF 2003). The sub-regional arrangements in London for such activities as skills training have also developed significantly since 1997, with organisations such as the West London Alliance taking on both an advocacy and service development role. Some argue that this may (Buck et al. 2002) have maintained their position by creating working arrangements with the mayor. It is also said that the GO for London is now larger that it was before the creation of the GLA (Jenkins 2004). From the point of view of London's citizens, communities, organisations, and businesses, the respective roles of the GLA and the mayor remain unclear.

The mayor's powers are growing with proposals published in 2006 (DCLG 2006d). The experience of the new London governance arrangements has been seen to be positive overall although the means by which the mayor is held to account through scrutiny and overview may be strengthened (Corry 2004a). This should include a review of the GO for London, that has an increasingly indistinct role (Walker 2004a), which is being further undermined by the increasingly joined-up approaches to delivery at the local level.

There are many views on the ways in which London-wide governance should develop in the future. There seems to be overall agreement that central government is retaining too many powers and purse strings centrally which could be more effectively managed at the London level (Travers 2004a; Walker 2004a). There is also a consensus that the current governance arrangements in London are too complex and difficult for people to understand. On other matters, there are opposing views such as the degree of financial autonomy open to the mayor where some argue that it needs to be wider to be more effective (Corry et al. 2004) while others take the opposing view. A further list of relationships and powers to be reviewed in the future include a range of suggestions from a GLA assembly member:

1   The relationship and the balance of powers between the Assembly and the mayor.
2   The relationship between the mayor, the Assembly and the London Boroughs.
3   Whether new powers and structures are needed to better manage sub-regional matters which currently sit midway between the Mayor and the boroughs.
4   Re-balancing the tax raising powers between government and the GLA in favour of the GLA, thereby raising its power and credibility.
5   Whether other areas such as for arts policy and regional housing funding, regional skills training could be devolved to the GLA.
6   Whether national rail services in London would be improved . . . by greater GLA/Transport for London involvement. (Biggs 2004, p. 20)

A second set of proposals has come from Tony Travers, a long-term commentator on London government and an academic (Travers 2004a)

1 To allow the mayor to appoint staff in alignment with the mayor's service responsibilities.
2 To review the mayor's power of appointment to the police and fire authorities and also to appoint the Commissioner of the metropolitan police (the Chief Constable) rather than the Home Secretary.
3 To allow the transfer of powers from Central government departments and also their power of appointment to the GLA. There could also be the transfer of civil servants to the GLA in order to implement a devolved solution.
4 The implementation of greater local fiscal autonomy similar to the arrangements in Scotland and Wales.
5 To provide London with a more effective form of city government which could come about through the implementation of the above reforms. (p. 53)

The mayor and the GLA are also reviewing the future of London's governance, with the mayor proposing that the future should lie in the restructuring of London to fewer boroughs.

Conclusions

The changes in regional and sub-regional governance arrangement which started in 1993 have had considerable effects on the way in which local authorities work with central government, other agencies, and each other. The emerging governance arrangements are also set to change these relationships further and this can be viewed as an area of emergent policy and practice – a work in progress, although the *Sub-National Economic Development and Regeneration Review* (HMT 2007) provides more indication of the development of sub-regions as delivery units, with possible governance changes to follow. In some cases, local authorities have been opposed to changes such as those in London or have seen the new bodies as generating more ineffectual layers of the central state that they have to deal with to manage. At the same time, the appointment of former local authority chief executives into regional government posts may have created a more open approach between central government and local authorities. Nevertheless, some local authorities take the view that those former local government officers appointed to central government regional posts now take a less sympathetic approach to local government.

14

WHAT IS THE FUTURE OF LOCAL GOVERNMENT?

Introduction

Although it seems strange to pose the question 'what is local government for?' more than a century after it was established, there is no single answer, although Lyons has now attempted to define its role more clearly (Lyons 2006). Local authorities have accreted functions and services which all have local delivery in common. These have often developed as a result of specific problems or events or local conditions. On the other hand, there have not been any specific guiding principles of what should or could be delivered locally. The choice of the tier of government to deliver each initiative is left to legislators and policy makers who have seen the specific outcome being pursued as being separate from the mode of delivery. Lyons (2006) has argued that this should now change and that local services should be the responsibility of local rather than central government. This would lead to and need an independent test of subsidiarity for government services and initiatives.

Thus, allocation of service delivery to a particular tier of government has been haphazard and serendipitous – without any serious consideration of the application of the principles of democracy, efficiency, or expertise. This may now be about to change. The role of the 'local' is now being considered from first principles, whether this is through new localism or through a wider effort to downsize central government, with a greater concentration on the 'front line' (OPSR 2003). Government has recognised that local government has made significant improvements in performance and delivery in the period since 1997. There is also a search for a longer term vision of the future for local government, stretching over the foreseeable future. In a speech in March 2004, the then local government Minister Nick Raynsford identified the challenges that go alongside achievement. He identified three unique characteristics of local government which are highly valued:

1 Local government is democratically accountable to local people
2 Local government is uniquely able to capture the importance of locality and place
3 Local government's ability to join up a wide range of services and providers and to build partnerships. (Raynsford 2004, p. 2)

This speech was followed by the announcement of a 10-year review of local government in July 2004 (ODPM 2004l). This chapter reviews the likely shaping influences on this debate on the future for local authorities and the prospects for local government and local governance.

Shaping influences for the future of local government

In addition to these trends which create cross-currents and tensions for the delivery of local governance in England there are also a number of important ideological elements to the debate which continue to have an impact as they develop and form, although at present it is difficult to assess their full impact.

Holding local government to account

Much of the debate about local government still revolves on its reliability and ability to deliver to an acceptable standard. Many in central government still do not believe that local government can deliver without being controlled. Yet systems have been instituted to externally validate the performance of local authorities such as CPA. Within local authorities, standards and scrutiny committees have been set up and the Standards Board for England has been created to independently review every complaint made against a councillor.

Local government is further held to account by the voluntary and community sector bodies which operate within the locality often as branches of national organisations such as the Citizen's Advice Bureau, Age Concern, Friends of the Earth, and the CPRE. These groups are often interested in specific issues such as age or medical conditions or the locality through neighbourhood or community groups. Greater transparency can lead to more open decision making that the community can see. Decisions made as a consequence of the community's priorities or through the Community Strategy are now shared more widely with community agencies in the LSP. At a government level, Zadek (2001) argues that NGOs are now acting as civil regulators, whereas NGOs acting within local communities become active members of civil partnerships and contribute to what he describes as new civil governance. These organisations also see their role as influencing the outcomes that they seek in three ways – through public pressure, offering technical or special expertise, and finally in legitimising outcomes.

Although Zadek is writing about NGOs at an international level, it is also possible to see these characteristics operating locally.

Reputation management

One of the main considerations for any private sector business is its 'brand' which is now seen to have an asset value in its own right. Local authorities have a 'lite' version of branding, with logos and themes which represent their core values or key programmes for their citizens, but major branding approaches are often not pursued by local authorities as they are seen to be 'wasteful'. One of the key exceptions to this branding approach occurs when any local authority is seeking to recruit a chief executive. This is an accepted point at which promote the local authority through advertisements, recruitment packs, and dedicated micro-web-sites. This kind of promotion is almost entirely aimed at local authority peers.

Reputation management is important at other times. During the period of discussion of local government boundary or structural reviews, as when unitary councils were created in the mid-1990s, the ability of a local authority to present its brand to its potential supporters is significant and as important within the potential boundaries of any new authority areas as in Parliament, central government, and other elite networks which are utilised to the maximum at these times.

However, there are also other types of reputation management which some local authorities develop in more systematic ways. The ability to be on easy terms with central government colleagues is often seen as a critical means of ensuring access to new initiatives or funding schemes, and successful local authorities manage these across a range of central government departments. These relationships are also important in dealing with crises before they occur and engendering trust. For some local authorities, the maintenance of these relationships is seen to be of critical importance to the reputation and functioning of the authority. In some local authorities, politicians have seen the way to achieve reputation management is through the recruitment of former members of the senior Civil Service to leading posts in order to open the doors to Whitehall.

In addition to the officers of the authority undertaking these roles, there are also seen to be other important political links. These can occur not only through organisations such as the LGA but also in the selection of an MP. Someone who has been an advisor to a minister or been well placed in a central government organisation can be seen as a considerable asset. These MPs, if tipped to be fast risers, can also bring some benefits to their constituency through informal channels as well as in more obvious ways. The ability to be able to put a local case is seen to be of essential importance in some areas. Although the local authority does not choose the candidate who stands for election as an MP, the local authority leaders are frequently amongst the most senior and influential politicians in their local parties and have a very strong role in their selection.

Finally, a key component of local authority reputation management is seen to be through the communication which local authorities have with their communities and citizens. Of those local authorities which were graded as excellent in the CPA process, a very high proportion scored well on the local communication component (Audit Commission and MORI 2003).

The choice agenda

The notion of choice has a long history, through its sponsorship from the Institute of Economic Affairs (Seldon et al. 2000) and Julian Le Grand, adviser to both the Thatcher and Blair governments (Le Grand 2004). Over a long period of time, the Conservative Party has considered the option of providing people with choice in services, with the option to provide education vouchers as one of the services discussed most frequently. The notion of choice has now become more main-stream in the consideration for government services as a whole with the consumer/customer/citizen/client being able to choose the provider of their service. This principle has been trialled in health, where, through the Choose and Book initiative, it has been possible for some patients to opt for treatment at another hospital after they have been on the waiting list for a specific period. In this model the funding for care follows the patient. The offer to the patient has been accompanied by transport to and from the hospital by taxi. The pilot projects have found a significant number of patients wiling to exercise this choice particularly for cataract and heart operations. The success of these experiments is both leading to their extension and also to the consideration of the wider application of this principle to their public services. As Wright and Ngao (2004, p. 4) point out, there is no reason why public services cannot apply 'good consumer principles' and also give more power to the user. However, they also point to the tension between the 'post-code' lottery for services, suggesting areas where national service standards or entitlement make more sense and others where a locally determined target is more appropriate. They do not indicate how the choice should be made between them.

Using the third sector

Since 1997, there has been a continuing interest in widening the base of agencies which deliver at the local level. Prior to 1997 this was seen to be primarily focused on the private sector, but since then charities have turned from a mix of voluntary agencies and service providers to more significant and direct players. This trans-formation was undertaken in the 1980s and 1990s by Housing Associations who retain social housing functions within diverse business organisations on a mixed charitable and company basis. Other charities are being encouraged in the same direction following papers on the role of 'intermediaries'.

The development of a local commissioning role (DCLG 2006a) suggests a more planned use of the community sector. In the past, the community sector would seek to respond to failures in public services by meeting particular needs – through welfare or particular age-related campaigning for children or the elderly.

The third sector role in this delivery is understood and rather than fund raising to support the needs of these overlooked groups or services, the community sector is more likely to be commissioned to specifically meet their needs within a local framework.

Whether the third sector will find such an approach acceptable is yet to be fully tested. There are also concerns about the range and quality of all local agencies, including those established with national framework. Volunteering is important as well as paid delivery and this agenda is still in a fluid state.

Smaller numbers of professionalised councillors?

Since 1997, the Labour government has initiated a variety of ways of electing and running local governance. It introduced proportional representation in Scotland, Wales, and London, and has mixed this system with a directly elected mayor in London. Proportional Representation (PR) is to be used in Scotland's local authorities from 2007. There have also been different means of voting introduced in England from postal voting to voting by phone and other electronic means. Councils have been restructured into executive and scrutiny members, with those in control able to exercise considerable power if their councils decide that this is the way in which they wish to be administered. This is set out in each council's constitution within the framework of the Local Government Act 2000. Councillors are now paid before enabling local political leaders to undertake this role as an equivalent of a salary.

The legacy of the 2000 changes has not yet been fully worked through in these areas and more change will emerge. What is clear is that the provisions of the Widdicombe Review (1986), which strongly discouraged the election of full-time councillors paid by other public bodies has been reinforced but has now been replaced by the recognition that local politics requires full-time leadership that should be adequately recompensed. What remains to be seen is whether councillors who act as local leaders or elected mayors will still view these roles as a stepping stone to Parliament or will see their roles at the local level to be more powerful.

One of the continuing concerns is that of voter apathy and the political mandate this undermines. Yet, there is also new evidence of interest in voting and other participatory styles of working. For popular votes, *Big Brother* has demonstrated that TV programmes can generate a mass vote. Warley has demonstrated the effects of a local campaign on electoral turnout and councillors elected and the Countryside March, and the fuel protests have demonstrated that new technology has had a major impact. For young people, often seen as politically apathetic, evidence also shows that they remain interested in political issues although they may wish to participate in modern ways. As Henn et al. found in 2002

Our research findings ... suggests that, although uninspired by, or even sceptical of, political parties and professional politicians, young people are sufficiently interested in political affairs to dispel the myth that they are apathetic and politically lazy. But they are also interested in a new style of politics. While they may eschew much of what could be characterised as 'formal' or conventional politics, they are interested in a different type of politics that is more participative and which focuses on localised, immediate issues. (Henn et al. 2002, p. 186)

Public service reform

One of the underlying features of the modernisation of local government has been the reform of public services. Reform of the public sector has partially been achieved through privatisation of utilities and public services such as gas, the Post Office and BT. Other parts of the government delivery machine have been established as agencies and this is still a favoured route for arms length delivery mechanisms that can be separated from ministers although the accountabilities still remain. The reform of the policy-making elements of the civil service has been more difficult despite a series of initiatives including proposals to decentralise (Lyons 2004), numerous speeches from cabinet secretaries at the beginning and end of their tenures (Sir Richard Wilson, Sir Andrew Turnbull, and Gus Macdonald) calling for more professionalisation, and greater experience of the outside world for senior appointments. None of these has yet generated any real changes.

Yet, the re-creation of the local state, based on a joined-up and integrated local public sector, with local authorities being given self-determination and the ability to run services currently delivered by central government could see more changes. Local government is now acknowledged to be better at delivery and more likely to manage its staff in an efficient and effective way. The push for public service reform could enable more joined-up delivery at a reduced cost. However, it will need major reform and transfer from Whitehall.

Creating a single public service

One of the major concerns for the future may be the nature of public service employment as a whole. At present, the public service, whether in health, teaching, local government, or central government, is divided by a number of organisational groupings. Although there are many similarities in terms and conditions and general pension arrangements, there are many specific differences, which have not been addressed so far. In local government, there has been a move to 'single status' employment, removing the differences between manual and non-manual workers so that the differences on hours of employment, leave entitlement, and other conditions are in the process of being removed at the local level. Where local authorities are working with health, particularly in the appointment of joint directors of Social Services and head of Primary Care Trusts or Heath Authorities, the arrangements have frequently become unstuck because these issues have not been properly agreed. Where local authorities are working directly with benefits staff in Job Centre Plus or in the delivery of Care Direct, the issues of terms and conditions are rarely addressed as again these are seen to be two separate services delivering shoulder to shoulder but not unifying. With the greater emphasis on integrated delivery it is hard to understand in the longer term how these issues can be overlooked.

One debate on this issue has started in the civil service, being led by the then Cabinet Secretary Sir Andrew Turnbull who argued that there should be no 'separate' civil service values, but rather those of the public service. In his article on the future of the civil service, David Walker (2003) writes questioning whether a civil service is needed at all, particularly one which is seen to be compartmentalised. In this piece, Walker states that

> Permanent Secretaries and council chief executives have different functions (the latter easier to specify and assess), but do they deserve to belong to different universes?
>
> Over a century and a half, we have been schooled in the belief that Whitehall is more important, that there is a special cadre of state officials who, because of their proximity to ministers, deserve higher consideration, more money, more medals, more status than the people 'out there'. It is as if there is an invisible pyramid stretching up to the Permanent Secretaries office. Most Permanent Secretaries find it hard enough to manage their own departments, let alone the service areas for which they are notionally responsible, yet those who are responsible are still regarded as inferior beings. (Walker 2003, p. 5)

Walker goes on to argue that a national service is required for human resources and finance and, in 2003, the Society of Local Authority Chief Personnel Officers, SOCPO, admitted civil servant members for the first time. Perhaps more significantly, the Cabinet Secretary announced with immediate effect in 2004 that the role of professionals at senior level would be re-introduced into the civil service, initially for areas such as Human Resources, contract and project management, finance, and IT (Turnbull 2004). This represented a significant reversal of civil service tradition introduced by the Northcote–Trevelyan reforms in 1854. In October 2003, Sir Andrew Turnbull speaking in Lisbon also raised the issue of the need for real reform in the civil service including confirmation of its impartiality (Timmins 2003).

Tony Blair took the opportunity of the 150th anniversary of the Northcote–Trevelyan Report, which has been seen to be the foundation for the modern civil service, to announce his proposed changes (Blair 2004). The new principle is a government which is organised around problems, not problems around departments. Government should have a smaller strategic centre, be open and be focused on outcomes. The pattern which is described is similar to that in local government and the voluntary sector where jobs are openly advertised, there is a strong delivery focus, and a small central core. However, this change in direction does not necessarily mean that the civil service culture, which is largely inward focused and more linked to the armed services in its thinking, will adapt to these changes rapidly.

The proposals for the creation of local public service boards and from the Gershon Efficiency Review to join up 'the front line' both lead to the debate on public service delivery being focused on the front line. As David Walker has commented, there was formerly no assumption that there was much in common between the posts of local authority chief executives, director of a primary care trust, or a director in the inland revenue but now these 'post-holders have a growing sense of identity. Working for the public, they all draw on an apparatus of law and . . . flows of funds from tax. Public service managers exercise . . . a special authority that stems from democratic decision making' (Walker 2004, p. 2).

Conclusions

A large combination of factors is now bearing down on the consideration of local government both now and in the future. The pressure for a more effective tier of local governance is becoming worldwide as the efficiency and democratic accountability arguments grow. At the same time, accountability and local choice of priorities are now being seen to have some direct links with electoral turnout. Where local issues are emerging through small local interest parties this is frequently leading to improvement in the turnout and democratic engagement. At the same time, there are pressures for uniformity of service standards as people feel uneasy about a post-code lottery for services in some areas, particularly for health care and prescribing practices, educational standards, and policing. In other areas, such as the provision of local facilities or parking measures, these are more local and although hotly contested are best resolved at this level.

There are some consistent roles that are emerging in the consideration of the future of local government which can be summarised as

- providing public sector focus across the community
- joining up public sector delivery across localities
- contributing to 'smaller' government
- having a general power of competence
- returning to the provision of locally generated funds to provide local services.

After all the reforms implemented since 1997, what is the future of local government? There have been improvements in performance, more freedoms and flexibilities, and different roles for councillors. There has also been a significant understanding that the funding provided to local authorities has been inadequate for the tasks they have to face. The efficiency requirements for local authorities will remain the same if not increase. At the same time, work by the Audit Commission (2003d) and the Treasury has shown that there has been significant under-funding in some areas such as health and education. There has also been an understanding that under-funding in these areas has led to a diversion of funds from other service areas such as transport, open spaces, sport, leisure, and libraries, which have other and connected consequences including those on health. As Dean (2004) states, 'Britain in the only country in Europe that is raising investment in health and education as a share of national income' and indeed has been criticised by the OECD for the speed of the increase in investment, which they conclude may damage its effective use. These criticisms may be based in part of the means of measuring productivity, which currently rests on simple input/output models. The Atkinson Review will look at new ways of measuring outcomes for policy and service recipients and measure these against inputs that may have some effect in this area.

Is this a renegotiated settlement for local government? There is no doubt that there is a movement to change the nature of the state at the local level. The accumulated impacts of the reforms identified in this book with those to come on local government finance amount to the most significant reform of local government since 1888. Historians and commentators will look back and see this as a 10-year revolution, although it is more difficult to comprehend from within its contemporary implementation.

There might also be a view that revealing the scale of local government reform would be enough to throw it off track. The public's continuing distrust and dissatisfaction with local government as a whole, rather than with the services it provides, can still endanger the amount of freedom that local authorities have. More localism means less centralism and the centre will want to protect its own. For local authorities, changes are never enough but the next opportunity may be to their own perceptions of what can be achieved. Local government has been given the context in which it can change and grow.

On the other hand, the repositioning of local governance has become a major challenge. The ability to 'blame' central government for unpopular actions or for genuinely difficult local budget choices has meant that politicians have always had a 'get out clause'. With local 'authority' comes new responsibility. Even within the pre-1997 system, local council leaders were perceived to have more power than MPs. In the new local government system this is even more the case.

How will local government cope with these changes? At present it is difficult to assess the key ways in which the implementation of further freedoms will evolve although some of the main trends could be

1 The establishment of a group of professional politicians at the local level which becomes separate from part time politicians.
2 A potential merger in some political and officer roles.
3 The creation of a local public expenditure budget merging local and central.
4 The creation of a local delivery programme between public sector agencies.
5 The cessation of central agency delivery of local services.
6 The creation of a targeted programme for improvement and change which will be set for five years.
7 A written constitution which provides the 'promise' to localities as well as the rules of operation.

8 The establishment of civic engagement in ways which have not been seen before such as digital TV for home voting.
9 The reduction of central government administrative costs and staff.
10 The preference of politicians to remain at the local and regional level rather than to enter Parliament.
11 Public agency delivery points at the local level.
12 The use of ATMs and phones for public service delivery and payments.

All of this implies a different kind of central state. The conceptualisation of the state has changed in the last decade from Foster's and Plowden's 'hollow state' in 1996 to one which is now involved in 'pushing' services to entitled citizens. There are significant moves to reduce the costs of delivering government but not to reduce what is delivered. Efficient delivery covers the costs of increased take up and can provide more public goods. Reducing back office costs in administration can deliver more service improvements or a wider service delivery to those in need.

Can this really occur? When the new local authorities were set up in the 1880s there was an assumption that municipalism would be a strong force at the local level and so it has been. However, concerns about the delivery of national standards and the effects of local policy choice when there are clearly delivery failures has led to a constant assumption that local government is not capable of delivering. The solution has been for central government to jump in. Why will this not occur again? The changing nature of the civil service is a central feature of the emerging settlement for local government – one cannot be changed without the other. The reforms of the civil service form a considerable package:

- Reintroduction of professional specialist to run certain function
- Regionalisation of functions
- Introduction of four year postings
- No job for life
- No senior role without external experience
- Management experience at a younger age. (Turnbull 2004)

These reforms are not enough to deal with a culture which has managed to retain its position against a variety of challenges over the years. Some departments have already taken pre-emptive strikes against these moves to provide themselves with greater control over budgets which were delivered by agencies, Defra and the countryside or by local authorities, or DfES and schools. If challenged, the empire strikes back. Yet, these changes are apparent in many other G8 countries including the United States and Canada. In Canada, the civil service has undertaken its own 'reform or die' programme which has delayed and changed fundamentally its role in government. Although the United Kingdom is not a federal state in the sense of the United States, Switzerland, or Germany, its new constitutional settlement which includes the local level creates the conditions for a smaller central state.

There is no doubt that local government is in a different place from where it was in 1997. It has been reformed, given greater autonomy, and can expect more in the future. Linklater (2006) describes Tony Blair as a great reforming prime minister on constitutional matters. This book has demonstrated that the reforms are significant and have created a modern local government that is growing to take its place as a partner in governance with the other democratically elected tiers of government in the United Kingdom.

Bibliography

Alesina A. and E. Spolaore (2003) *The Size of Nations*. London: MIT Press.

Allmendinger P., M. Tewdwr-Jones, and J. Morphet (2003, October) New order – planning and local government reforms. *Town and Country Planning*: 274–277.

Amin A., D. Massey, and N. Thrift (2003) *Decentering the Nation: A Radical Approach to Regional Inequality*. London: Catalyst.

Anderson O. (1937) *Rotten Borough*. London: Fourth Estate.

Apostolakis C. (2004) Citywide and local strategic partnerships in urban regeneration: can collaboration take things forward. *Politics* 24(2): 103–112.

Ashworth R. (2003) *Evaluating the Effectiveness of Local Scrutiny Committees*. Swindon: ESRC Research report on grant R000223542.

Audit Commission (1990) *We Can't Go on Meeting Like This*. London: Audit Commission.

Audit Commission (2002a) *Recruitment and Retention – A Public Service Workforce for the Twentieth Century*. London: Audit Commission.

Audit Commission (2002b) *Quality of Life Using Quality of Life Indicators*. London: Audit Commission.

Audit Commission (2002c) *Connecting with Citizens and Users*. London: Audit Commission.

Audit Commission (2002d) *Message beyond the Medium Improving Local Government Services through e-Government in England*. London: Audit Commission.

Audit Commission (2002e) *The Final CPA Assessment Framework for Single Tier and County Councils*. London: Audit Commission.

Audit Commission (2003a) *Connecting with Users and Citizens*. London: Audit Commission.

Audit Commission (2003b) *Learning from CPA*. London: Audit Commission.

Audit Commission (2003c) *CPA – The Way Forward Single Tier and County Councils*. London: Audit Commission.

Audit Commission (2003d) *Strategic Regulation: Minimising the Burden, Minimising the Impact*. London: Audit Commission.

Audit Commission (2003e) *Council Tax Increases 2003–4: Why Were They So High?* London: Audit Commission.

Audit Commission (2004a) *People, Places and Prosperity*. London: Audit Commission.

Audit Commission (2004b) *CPA Key Lines of Enquiry for Corporate Assessment Practitioner Version*. London: Audit Commission.

Audit Commission and MORI (2003) *Trust in Public Institutions*. London: MORI.

Bache I. (2003) Governing through governance: education policy control under new labour. *Political Studies* 51(2): 300–314.

Bains Report (1972) *The Structure and Management of Local Government*. London: HMSO.

Balls E. (2003) Foreword in 'new localism'. In D. Corry and G. Stoker (eds). London: New Local Government Network.

Beecham J. (2005) Letter to *The Guardian*, 6 January.

Benington J., L. de Groot, and J. Foot (2006) *Lest We Forget: Democracy, Neighbourhoods and Government*. London: Solace Imprint Foundation.

Betjeman J. (1958) *Collected Poems*. London: John Murray.

Bevan M. (2003) *New Parish and Town Councils in Urban Areas Communities and DIY Democracy*. York: JRF.

Bichard M. (2004) *The Bichard Inquiry Report*. London: The House of Commons.

Biggs J. (2004) The London Assembly Member. In Corry (ed.), op cit, , pp. 17–20.

Birmingham City Council (2003) *The Birmingham City-Region Creating a Distinctive European City-Region. A First Prospectus for Enhancing the Competitiveness and Renaissance of the Birmingham City Region*. Birmingham: Birmingham City Council.

Blackburn with Darwen Council (2003) Governance paper – 'LSPs with teeth' Blackburn with Darwen Council. October Innovations Forum, www.ODPM.gsi.gov.uk

Black Country Consortium (2003) *Looking Forward: The Black Country in 2033*. Sandwell: Black Country Consortium.

Blair T. (2002) The courage of our convictions: why reform of the public services is the route to social justice? *Fabian Ideas 603*. London: The Fabian Society.

Blair T. (2004) Reform of the Civil Service, 24 February, www.number-10.gov.uk

Blears H. (2003) *Communities in Control Public Services and Local Socialism*. London: The Fabian Society.

Braine J. (1957) *Room at the Top*. Harmondsworth: Penguin.

Bruce-Lockhart S. (2005, February) New Local Government Network Conference on Regions.

Buck N., I. Gordon, P. Hall, M. Harloe, and M. Kleinman (2002) *Working Capital Life and Labour in Contemporary London*. London: Routledge.

Burgess P., S. Hall, J. Mawson, and G. Pearce (2001) *Devolved Approaches to Local Governance Policy and Practice in Neighbourhood Management*. York: JRF.

Byatt I. (2001) *Delivering Better Services for Citizens Local Government Procurement Taskforce*. London: ODPM.

Cabinet Office (1999) *Modernising Government*. London: HMSO.

Cabinet Office (2000*) e.gov Electronic Government Services for the 21st Century*. London: Performance and Innovation Unit.

Cabinet Office (2001) *Better Policy Delivery and Design: A Discussion Paper*. London: Performance and Innovation Unit/Cabinet Office.

Cabinet Office (2003) *Social Capital*. London: Cabinet Office.

Cabinet Office (2005) *Strategic Audit of the UK*. London: Cabinet Office.

Cabinet Office/e-government Unit (2005) *Transformational Government Strategy*. London: Cabinet Office.

Cantle T. (2002) *Community Cohesion*. London: The Home Office.

Carvel J. (2006) Memberships soar as average Briton joins 17 organisations. *Guardian Unlimited*, 7 November.

Chadwick A., J. Glasson, H. Lawton Smith, G. Clark, and J. Simmie (2003) *Enterprising Oxford: The Anatomy of the Oxfordshire High-Tec Economy*. Oxford: Oxfordshire Economic Observatory/Oxford University.

Cherry G. (1994*) Birmingham: A Study in Geography, History and Planning*. Chichester: John Wiley & Sons.

Cochrane A., J. Peck, and A. Tickell (2002) Olympic dreams: Vision of partnership. In Peck and Ward (eds), op cit, pp. 95–115.

Commission for Local Democracy (1995) *Taking Charge: The Rebirth of Local Democracy*. London: Municipal Journal Books.

Commission of the European Communities (2002) *Draft Paper on Benchmarking Citizen Transactions*. Brussels: Commission of the European Communities.

Commission of the European Communities (2003) *eEurope*. Brussels: Commission of the European Communities.

Commission of the European Communities (2007) *The Community Strategic Guidelines on Cohesion 2007–2013*. Brussels: Commission of the European Communities.

Committee Standards in Public Life (1998) Fifth Report of the Committee on Standards in Public Life, Chairman Lord Neill, Cm 4057–1.

Corry D. (2003) The Brown–Milburn frontline. *The Guardian*, 6 March.

Corry D. (ed.) (2004a) *London Calling Reflections on Four Years of the GLA and Solutions for the Future*. London: New Local Government Network.

Corry D. (2004b) London's governance today. In Corry (ed.) op cit, pp. 9–12.

Corry D. and G. Stoker (2002) *New Localism*. London: New Local Government Network.

Corry D. and G. Stoker (2003) *New Localism Refashioning the Centre–Local Relationship*. London: New Local Government Network.

Corry D., W. Hatter, I. Parker, A. Randle, and G. Stoker (2004) *Joining-Up Local Democracy Governance Systems for New Localism*. London: New Local Government Network.

Council of Europe (1985) *European Charter of Self-Government*. Strasbourg: Council of Europe, 15: x.

Creative Cultures (2004) *Draft Guidance on Integrating Cultural and Community Strategies*. London: Department of Culture, Media and Sport.

Crouch C. (2000) Coping with Post-democracy. *Fabian Ideas 598*. London: The Fabian Society.

Cunningham C. (1981) *Victorian and Edwardian Town Halls*. London: Routledge and Kegan Paul.

Davis H., J. Downe, and S. Martin (2004) *The Changing Role of Audit Commission Inspection of Local Government*. York: JRF.

DCA (2003a) *Privacy and Data Sharing Survey of Public Awareness and Perceptions*. London: Department for Constitutional Affairs.

DCA (2003b) *Privacy and Data Sharing. The Way Forward*. London: Department for Constitutional Affairs.

DCLG (2006a) *Strong and Prosperous Communities Local Government White Paper*, vols 1 and 2. London: Department of Communities and Local Government.

DCLG (2006b) *Developing the Local Government Services Market to Support the Long Term Strategy for Local Government*. London: CLG.

DCLG (2006c) *Local Area Agreements Research: Round 2 Negotiations and Early Progress in Round 1*. London: CLG.

DCLG (2006d) *The Role of City Development Companies in English Cities and City-Regions.* London: CLG.

DCLG (2006e) *GLA Bill.* London: CLG.

DCMS (2000) *Creating Opportunities: Guidance for Local Authorities on Cultural Strategies.* London: Department of Culture, Media and Sport.

Dean M. (2004) Opinion: the need to review the way we measure public services, *Society Guardian*, 4 February, p. 5.

DETR (1998, July) *Modern Local Government: In Touch with the People.* Cmnd 4014.

DETR *Local Government Act 1999* . London: HMSO.

DETR (2000a) *Best Value Performance Indicators.* London: DETR.

DETR (2000b) *Local Government Act.* London: HMSO.

DETR (2001a) *Supporting Strategic Service Delivery Partnerships in Local Government – A Research and Development Programme.* London: DETR.

DETR (2001b, March 15) *Local Government Act 1999 Section 19 Best Value and Procurement: Handling of Workforce Matters in Contracting.* London: DETR.

DETR (2001c) *Local Strategic Partnerships Goavernment Guidance.* London: DETR.

DETR (2002) *e-gov@local Draft National Strategy for Local e-Government.* London: DETR.

DfES (2003) *Every Child Matters.* London: DfES.

Doherty B., M. Paterson, A. Plows, and D. Wall (2003) Explaining the fuel protests. *British Journal of Politics and International Relations* 5(1): 1–23.

DTLR (2000) *Modernising Local Government Finance: A Green Paper.* London: DTLR.

DTLR (2001a) *Access for All Modern Councils Modern Services.* London: DTLR.

DTLR (2001b) *Guidance on Preparing Community Strategies.* London: DTLR.

DTLR (2001c) *A New Commitment to Neighbourhood Renewal – National Strategy Action Plan.* London: DTLR.

DTLR (2001d) *Strong Local Leadership – Quality Public Services.* London: DTLR

Eddington, Rod, Sir (2007) *Transport's Role in Sustaining UK's Productivity and Competitiveness: The Case for Action.* London: Her Majesty's Treasury.

Ellwood S., S. Nutley, M. Tricker, and P. Waterston (1992) *Parish and Town Councils in England: A Survey.* London HMSO.

English Nature (1998) *Natural Areas Boundaries.* Peterborough: English Nature.

Entec (2003) *The Relationships between Community Strategies and Local Development Frameworks Final Report.* London: ODPM.

Entwistle T., L. Dowson, and J. Law (2003) *Changing to Improve: Ten Case Studies from the Evaluation of the Best Value Regime.* London: ODPM.

Flinders M. (2002) Shifting the balance? Parliament, the Executive and the British Constitution. *Political Studies* 50(1): 23–42.

Foster C.D. and F.J. Plowden (1996) *The State under Stress Can the Hollow State Be Good Government.* Buckingham: Open University Press.

Fothergill S. (1994) The impact of regional alliances: the case of the EU coalfields. *European Urban and Regional Studies* 1(2): 177–180.

Gavin N.T. and D. Sanders (2003) The Press and its Influence on British Political Attitudes Under New Labour, *Political Studies* 51(3): 573–91.

Geddes M. (2004) *Local Strategic Partnerships.* London: ODPM.

Gershon P. (2004) *Releasing Resources to the Frontline: Independent Review of Public Sector Efficiency.* London: Her Majesty's Treasury.

Giddens A. (1998) *The Third Way: The Renewal of Social Democracy.* Cambridge: Polity Press.

Goodin R.E. and S.J. Niemeyer (2003) When does deliberation begin? Internal reflection versus public discussion in deliberative democracy. *Political Studies* (51): 627–649.

Graham S. (2002) Bridging urban digital divides? Urban polarisation and information and communication technologies (ICTs). *Urban Studies* 39(1): 33–56.

Greer A. and P. Hoggett (1996) Quangos and local governance. In Pratchett and Wilson (eds), pp. 150–169.

Grieco M. (2000) Intelligent urban development: the emergence of 'wired' government and administration guest editor's introduction. *Urban Studies* 37(10): 1719–1721.

Gyford J. (1991) *Citizens, Consumers and Councils Local Government and the Public.* Basingstoke: Macmillan.

Harper R. (2002) *The Measurement of Social Capital in the United Kingdom.* London: ONS.

Headrick J.E. (1962) *The Town Clerk in English Local Government.* London: George Allen & Unwin.

Henn M., M. Weinstein, and D. Wring (2002) A generation apart? Youth and political participation in Britain. *British Journal of Politics and International Relations* 4(2): 167–192.

Hewison G. (2001) A power of general competence – should it be granted to local government in New Zealand? *Auckland University Law Review* 9(2): 498–528.

HMT (2002) *The Role of the Voluntary and Community Sector in Service Delivery: A Cross Cutting Review.* London: HMT.

HMT (2004a) *Public Service Agreements White Paper.* London: HMT.

HMT (2004b) *Devolved Decision Making: 1 Delivering Better Public Services: Refining Targets and Performance Management.* London: HMT.

HMT (2004c) *Devolved Decision Making: 2 Meeting the Regional Economic Challenge: Increasing Regional and Local Flexibility.* London: HMT.

HMT (2004d), *Review of Civil Procurement in Central Government,* known as *The Gershon Report.* London: HMT.

HMT (2006) *Devolved Decision Making: 3 Cities.* London: HMT.

HMT (2007) *Sub-National Economic Development and Regeneration Review.* London: HMT.

HMT and ODPM (2003) *Productivity in the UK 4 – The Local Dimension.* London: HMT.

Holtby W. (1936/1988) *South Riding.* London: Virago.

Home Office (nd1) *Consultation and Policy Appraisal: A Code of Good Practice.* London: The Home Office.

Home Office (nd2) *Compact Code of Good Practice on Community Groups.* London: The Home Office.

Home Office (nd3) *Compact on Relations between Government and the Voluntary Sector in England.* London: The Home Office.

Home Office (nd4) *Black and Minority Ethnic Voluntary and Community Organisations: A Code of Good Practice.* London: The Home Office.

Hughes M., C. Skelcher, P. Jas, and P. Whiteman (2004) *Learning from Experience of Recovery Paths to Recovery: 2nd Annual Report.* London: ODPM.

Illsley B, M.G. Lloyd, and B. Lynch (1999) One stop shops in Scotland: diversity in co-ordination and integration? *Local Governance* 25(4): 201–210.

Imrie R. and M. Raco (2003) *Urban Renaissance? New Labour, Community and Urban Policy.* Bristol: Policy Press.

Jenkins S. (2004) Foreword. In D. Corry (ed.), op cit, p. 5.

Johnson K. and W. Hatter (nd) *Realising the Potential of Scrutiny*. London: New Local Government Network and Centre for Public Scrutiny.

Jones G. and T. Travers (1996) Central government perceptions of local government. In Pratchett and Wilson (eds), op cit, pp. 84–105.

Kakabadse A., N. Korac-Kakabadse, and A. Kouzmin (2003) Ethics, values and behaviours: comparison of three case studies examining the paucity of leadership in government. *Public Administration* 81(3): 477–508.

Keating M., J. Loughlin, and K. Deschouwer (2003) *Culture, Institutions and Economic Development: A Study of Eight European Regions*. Camberley: Edward Elgar.

Kelly J. (2003) The Audit Commission: guiding, steering and regulating local government. *Public Administration* 81(3): 459–476.

Kent CC (2003) *Governance Paper 'LSPs with Teeth' Kent Model, October*. London: ODPM Innovations Forum, www.ODPM.gov.uk

Kitchin H. (1996) A power of general competence for local government. In Pratchett and Wilson (eds), op cit, pp. 210–228.

Knox C. (2002) *Local Government Administration*. University of Ulster Paper for the Review of Public Administration in Northern Ireland. Belfast: University of Ulster.

Knox M. with D. Alcock, A. Roderick, and J. Iles (2002) *Approaches to Community Governance: Models for Mixed Tenure Communities*. York: The Policy Press.

Laming H. (2003) *The Victoria Climbie Inquiry Report*. London: Department of Health.

Lawless P. (1989) *Britain's Inner Cities*, 2nd edn. London: Paul Chapman.

Lawton Smith H., J. Glasson, J. Simmie, A. Chadwick, and G. Clark (2003) *Enterprising Oxford: The Growth of the Oxfordshire High-Tec Economy*. Oxford: Oxfordshire Economic Observatory/Oxford University.

Layton J. (2004) Incremental approaches to partnership. In Southwood (ed.), op cit, pp. 28–30.

LBHF (2003) Governance Paper 'LSPs with teeth' – Hammersmith and Fulham Paper to the October Innovations Forum, www.ODPM.gov.uk

Leach S., C. Skelcher, C. Lloyd-Jones, C. Copus, E. Dunstan, D. Hall, et al. (2003) *Strengthening Local Democracy Making the Most of the Constitution*. London ODPM.

Le Grand J. (2004) *Targets Voice or Choice* http://www.odi.org.uk/speeches/public_service_delivery_2004/meeting_24nov/legrand.pdf

Lent A. and N. Arend (2004) *Making Choices: How Can Choice Improve Local Public Services?* London: New Local Government Network.

LGA (2003a, May) Regional governance: a survey of local authorities. *Research Briefing 3.03*. London: LGA.

LGA (2003b) Ambition thwarted. *LGA Summer Review*. London: LGA.

LGA (2003c) *Designs on Democracy Case Studies on Democratic Participation*. London: LGA.

LGA (2004) *Local Public Service Boards: An Innovation Forum Prospectus*. London: LGA.

Liddle J. and A. Townsend (2003) Reflections on the development of local strategic partnerships: key emerging issues. *Local Governance* 29(1): 37–54.

Ling T. (2002) Delivering joined up government in the UK: dimensions, issues and problems. *Public Administration* 80(4): 615–642.

Linklater M. (2006), Blair's legacy shining, *The Scotsman*, 19 November.

Loughlin J. (2001a) *Subnational Democracy in the European Union Challenges and Opportunities*. Oxford: Oxford University Press.

Loughlin J. (2001b) *The United Kingdom: From Hypercentralization to Devolution*. Oxford: Oxford University Press, pp. 37–60.

Loughlin J. and S. Martin (2003) *International Lessons on Balance of Funding*. Cardiff: Cardiff University Centre for Local and Regional Government Research.

Loughlin M. (1996) The constitutional status of local government. In Pratchett and Wilson (eds), op cit.

Lucas K., A. Ross, and S. Fuller (2003) *What's In a Name? Local Agenda 21, Community Planning and Neighbourhood Renewal*. York: JRF.

Lyons M. (2004) *Independent Review of Public Sector Relocation 'Well placed to Deliver? – Shaping the Pattern of Government Service'*. London: HMT.

Lyons M. (2006) *National Prosperity, Local Choice and Civic Engagement: A New Partnership between Central and Local Government for the 21st Century*. London: HMT.

Macdonald K. (2003) *How Regeneration Partnerships Learn and Develop*. York: JRF.

Macintosh A., E. Robson, E. Smyth, and A. Whyte (2003) Electronic participation and young people. *Social Science Computer Review* 21(1): 43–54.

Mandelson P. and R. Liddle (1996) *The Blair Revolution: Can New Labour Deliver?* London: Faber & Faber.

Marsh P.T. (1994) *Joseph Chamberlain Entrepreneur in Politics*. London: Yale University Press.

Martin, S. (2000) Implementing best value: local public services in transition. *Public Administration* 78(1): 209–227.

Mathur N., C. Skelcher, and M. Smith (2004) *Effective Partnership and Good Governance: Conformance or Performance*, ESRC Project Final Report. Birmingham: University of Birmingham, Inlogov.

McGregor A., A. Glass, K. Higgins, L. Macdougall, and V. Sutherland (2003) *Developing People – Regenerating Place: Achieving Greater Integration for Local Area Regeneration*. York: The Policy Press.

McLaverty P. (1996) *The Politics of Empowerment*. Aldershot: Dartmouth.

McLean I. and A. McMillan (2003) *New Localism, New Finance*. London: New Local Government Network.

Milburn A. (2003) *The Guardian*, 26 September, p. 1.

Milburn A. (2005, February) A four-step plan to wrest power from the state to the citizen. *Public*: 30–31.

Miliband D. (2005, May 20) Civic pride for the modern age speech to the Core Cities Group. London: CLG.

Miliband D. (2006a, February 21) Double devolution. *The Guardian*.

Miliband D. (2006b, July 4) Double devolution LGA conference.

Moreira G. (2003, April 9–11) *E-Government at the Local Level in Portugal*. Oxford: Planning Research Conference Oxford Brookes University.

Morphet J. (1990) Can we save open space? *ECOS* 11(4): 27–34.

Morphet J. (1993a) *The Role of the Chief Executive in Local Government*. Harlow: Longman.

Morphet J. (1993b) *Towards Sustainability A Guide for Local Authorities*. Luton: Local Government Management Board.

Morphet J. (1994) Committee of the regions. *Local Government Policy Making* 20(5).

Morphet J. (2003a) Joining policy with implementation in central government: the approach to e-government. *Local Government Studies* 29(1): 111–116.

Morphet J. (2003b) *Understanding e-government*. London: Chadwick House.

Morphet J. (2004a, September) New localism. *Town and Country Planning*.

Morphet J. (2004b, April) New localism, paper to Planning Research Conference. Aberdeen.

Morphet J. (2004c) *Integration in Planning*. London: Royal Town Planning Institute.

Morphet J. and H. Brougham (1990, March) The planning consequences of the community charge. *Town and Country Planning*.

Mulgan G. (2004) Foreword. In Corry et al. (eds), op cit, pp. 6–7.

Mulholland H. (2004, May 26) The man in the middle. *The Guardian*, society section.

Murray M. and J. Greer (2002) Participatory planning as dialogue: The Northern Ireland regional strategic framework and its public examination process. *Policy Studies* 23(3/4): 191–209.

ODPM (2002a) *Structures for Partnerships Technical Notes Strategic Partnering Taskforce*. London: ODPM.

ODPM (2003a) *Guidance on Best Value Performance Plans: A Consultation Paper*. London: ODPM.

ODPM (2003b) *Guidance on Establishing Business Improvement Districts*. London: ODPM.

ODPM (2003c) *Draft Planning Policy Statement: Local Development Frameworks*. London: ODPM.

ODPM (2003d) *Review of Area Based Initiatives Impacts and Outcomes*. London: Regional Coordination Unit.

ODPM (2003e) *Local Government White Paper, Strong Local Leadership – Quality Public Services CM 5237, Implementation Plan*. London: ODPM.

ODPM (2003f) *Review of Area Based Initiatives Impacts and Outcomes*. London: Regional Coordination Unit.

ODPM (2003g) *A National Strategy for Local e-Government*. London: ODPM.

ODPM (2003h) *Your Region Your Choice*. London: ODPM.

ODPM (2003i) *Polycentricity Scoping Study*. London: ODPM.

ODPM (2003j) *Rethinking Service Delivery Volume 1: An Introduction to Strategic Delivery Partnerships*. London: ODPM.

ODPM (2003k) *Rethinking Service Delivery Volume 2: From Vision to Outline Business Case*. London: ODPM.

ODPM (2003l) *Removing Plan Requirements Consultation Paper*. London: ODPM.

ODPM (2003m) *Planning Policy Statement 11 Regional Spatial Strategies*. London: ODPM.

ODPM (2003n) *Government Response to ODPM Select Committee Report on Reducing Regional Disparities*. London: ODPM.

ODPM (2003o) *Implementing Electronic Government 3 Annual Return*. London: ODPM.

ODPM (2004a) Competitive European cities: where do the core cities stand? *Urban Research Summary* no. 13. London: ODPM.

ODPM (2004b) *Guidance on Best Value Performance Plans*. London: ODPM.

ODPM (2004c) *The Future of Local Government Local-Vision in Partnership with Local Government*. London: ODPM.

ODPM (2004d) *Strategic Partnering Taskforce Final Report*. London: ODPM.

ODPM (2004e) *Defining E-Government Outcomes for 2005 to Support the Priority Services and National Transformation Agenda for Local Authorities in England 'Priority Outcomes for Local e-Government'*. London: ODPM.

ODPM (2004f, July 13) Raynsford welcomes continued investment in local services. *Press Notice* 2004/0163.

ODPM (2004g, May 19) EU procurement directives statistical returns for 2003 letter to local authority chief executives.

ODPM (2004h) *The Draft Environmental Assessment of Plans and Programmes Regulations 2004 EU/2001/42/EC*. London: ODPM.

ODPM (2004i) *Evaluation of Local Strategic Partnerships Governance: A Briefing Note for LSPs by LSPs*. London: ODPM.

ODPM (2004j) *Evaluation of Local Strategic Partnerships: Mainstreaming: A Briefing Note by LSPs for LSPs*. London: ODPM.

ODPM (2004k) *Local Area Agreements: A Prospectus*. London: ODPM.

ODPM (2004l) *The Future of Local Government: Developing a Ten Year Vision*. London: ODPM.

ODPM (2004m) *Implementing Electronic Government Statement 4 Annual Return*. London: ODPM.

ODPM (2005a) *People, Places and Prosperity Five Year Plan*. London: ODPM.

ODPM (2005b) *Sustainable Communities*. London: ODPM.

ODPM (2005c) *Civic Engagement and Public Services: Why Neighbourhoods Matter*. London: ODPM.

ODPM (2005d) *Vibrant Local Leadership*. London: ODPM.

ODPM (2005e) *Local Strategic Partnerships Shaping Their Future Consultation Paper*. London: ODPM.

ODPM (2005f) *Press Notice* 2005/0193. London: ODPM.

ODPM and Employers Organisation (2003) *Pay and Workforce Strategy for Local Government*. London: ODPM.

ODPM, HMT, and DTI (2003) *Cities, Regions and Competitiveness Second Report from the Working Party of Government Departments, the Core Cities and the RDAs*. London: ODPM.

ODPM, HMT, and DTI (2004) *Regional Growth Frontier Economics*. London: ODPM.

ODPM/Innovation Forum (2003) Innovation Forum (October) www.communities.gov.uk

ODPM/LGA (2003) *Local Public Service Agreements Second Generation*. London: ODPM.

ODPM/RCU (2002) *Review of Area Based Initiatives*. London: ODPM.

OECD (1992) *Regulatory Reform, Privatisation and Competition*. Paris: OECD.

Office of Public Management (2003) *Mapping Approaches to Integrating Performance Indicators across Local Strategic Partnerships Gathering Examples of Perceived Good Practice*. London: Office of Public Management.

Office of Public Service Reform (2004) *Inspecting for Improvement Developing a Customer Focused Approach*. London: Cabinet Office.

Office of Government Commerce (2006, December 8) Local government on course to meet Gershon efficiency targets one year early. *Press Notice*, www.ogc.gov.uk

OPSR (2002) *Reforming our Public Services Principles into Practice*. London: Cabinet Office.

Osborne D. and T. Gaebler (1992) *Reinventing Government*. Reading: Addison-Wesley.

Osborne D. and P. Hutchinson (2004) *The Price of Government*. New York: Basic Books.

Osterland M. (1994) Coping with democracy: the re-institution of local self government in eastern Germany. *European Urban and Regional Studies* 1(1): 5–17.

O2C Arc (2003) *The Spirit of Innovation*, www.oxford2cambridge.net

Pattie C.J. and R.J. Johnston (2005) Electoral participation and political context: the turnout/marginality paradox at the 2001 British General Election. *Environment and Planning A* 37(7): 1191–1206.

Pattie C.J., P. Seyd and P. Whiteley (2003). Citizenship and civic engagement: attitudes and behaviour in Britain. *Political Studies* 51(3): 443–468.

Peck J. and K. Ward (eds) *City of Revolution. Restructuring Manchester.* Manchester: Manchester University Press.

Perri 6, D. Leat, K. Seltzer, and G. Stoker (1999) *Governing in the Round Strategies for Holistic Government.* London: Demos.

Perri 6, D. Leat, K. Selzer, and G. Stoker (2002) *Towards Holistic Governance: The New Reform Agenda.* Basingstoke: Palgrave.

Peterson H. (2004) *LSPs with teeth London.* London: Local Government Association.

Pickvance C. (1991) The difficulty of control and the ease of structural reform: British local government in the 1980s. In Pickvance and Preteceille (eds), op cit, pp. 48–88.

Pickvance C. and E. Preteceille (eds) (1991a) *State Restructuring and Local Power: A Comparative Perspective.* London: Pinter.

Pickvance C. and E. Preteceille (eds) (1991b) Introduction. In Pickvance and Preteceille (eds), op cit, pp. 1–17.

Pinfield G. and J. Saunders (2000) Community strategies and LA21 strategies. *EG Promoting Local Sustainable Development* 6(8): 15–18.

Pollitt C. (2003) Joined up government: a survey. *Political Studies Review* 1: 34–49.

Portfolio Communications (2003) *The Take Up of E-Government Services.* London: ICM Ltd.

Pratchett L. and D. Wilson (eds) *Local Democracy and Local Government.* Basingstoke: Macmillan.

Pratchett L. and M. Wingfield (1996) The demise of the public service ethos. In Pratchett and Wilson (eds), op cit, pp. 106–126.

PriceWaterHouseCoopers LLP (2004) *The Role of Staff in Delivering High Quality Public Services.* London: ODPM.

Putnam R. (1993) *Making Democracy Work: Civic Traditions in Modern Italy.* Princeton, NJ: Princeton University Press.

Putnam R. (2000) *Bowling Alone.* London: Simon & Schuster.

Putnam Robert D. and Lewis Feldstein (with Don Cohen) (2003) *Better Together, Restroring the Americal Community*, New York: Simon & Schuster.

Quirk B. (2001) *Esprit de Corps: Leadership for Progressive Change in Local Government.* York: JRF.

Quirk B. and ODPM letter to local authority chief executives on implementing efficiency, April 2005, www.communities.gov.uk

Rallings. C, M. Temple, and M. Thrasher (1996) Participation in local elections. In Pratchett and Wilson (eds), op cit, pp. 62–83.

Rallings C., M. Thrasher, and R. Johnston (2002) The slow death of a governing party: the erosion of conservative local electoral support in England 1979–97. *British Journal of Politics and International Relations* 4(2): 271–298.

Raynsford N. (2004, March 15) Speech to *Local Government Chronicle*, Policy Forum, www.communities.gov.uk

Redditch Partnership (2003) *20:20 Vision Community Strategy for the Borough of Redditch Summary Version*. Redditch: Redditch Borough Council.

Richard I. (2004) *Report of the Richard Commission on the Powers and Electoral Arrangements of the National Assembly for Wales*. Cardiff: The Richard Commission.

Sanderson I., S. Martin, and L. Dowson (2004) *Beyond Performance Management? Evaluation for Effective Local Governance*, ESRC End of Award Report. Swindon: ESRC.

Sandford M. (2004a) *Strategic Regional Government: Lessons from London*. London: Public Management and Policy Association/The Constitution Unit.

Sandford M. (2004b) Elected Mayors I: Political Innovation, Electoral Systems and Revitalising Democracy, *Local Government Studies*, March, 30(1): 1–21.

Seldon A., G. Tullock, and G.L. Brady (2000) *A Primer in Public Choice*. London: Institute of Economic Affairs.

Slater S. (2003, July/August) Regions: when the difference matter in regions to be cheerful. *Green Futures Regional Futures:* i–ii.

Slaughter A. (2004) Working with the best. In Corry (ed.), op cit, pp. 21–24.

Smith G. and C. Wales (2000) Citizens juries and deliberative democracy. *Political Studies* 48: 51–65.

Snape S. and S. Leach (2002) *The Development of Overview and Scrutiny in Local Government*. London: ODPM.

Southwood E. (ed.) (2004) *Procurement and Partnership Doing It Right. Making It Work*. London: New Local Government Network.

Staffordshire County Council (nd) *The Community Strategy for Staffordshire*. Stafford: Staffordshire County Council.

Stern N. (2006) *The Economics of Climate Change*. London: HMT.

Stewart J. (1995) A future for local authorities as community government. In Stewart and Stoker (eds), op cit, pp. 249–267.

Stewart J. (1996) Reforming the new magistracy. In Pratchett and Wilson (eds), op cit.

Stewart J. and G. Stoker (eds) (1995) *Local Government in the 1990s*. London: Macmillan.

Stoker G. (ed.) (1999) *The New Management of British Local Government*. Basingstoke: Macmillan.

Stoker G. (2004) *Transforming Local Governance from Thatcherism to New Labour*. Basingstoke: Palgrave Macmillan.

Stoker G. (2005) *What Is Local Government For? Refocusing Local Governance to Meet the Challenges of the 21st Century*. London: New Local Government Network.

Stoker G., F. Gains, P. John, N. Rao, and A. Harding (2003) *Implementing the 2000 Act with Respect to New Council Constitutions and the Ethical Framework First Report*. Manchester: ODPM.

Storey D. (1960) *This Sporting Life*. London: Longmans.

Strachan J. (2004, July 10) Closing Speech Local Government Association Conference. Bournemouth.

Sunderland (2003, October) Discussion paper – integrated public services innovation forum, Sunderland Council, www.ODPM.gov.uk

Sweeting D. and H. Ball (2002) Overview and scrutiny of leadership: the experience of Bristol City Council. *Local Governance* 28(3): 201–212.

Taylor M. (2002) *Top Down Meets Bottom Up Neighbourhood Management*. York: JRF.

Timmins N. (2003) Whitehall warned over public sector reputation. *Financial Times*, 24 October, p. 2.

Toynbee P. (2004) The naked kleptocracy that leads Britain's private sector. *The Guardian*, December 8.

Travers T. (2004a) *The Politics of London – Governing an Ungovernable City*. Basingstoke: Palgrave Macmillan.

Travers T. (2004b) Future agenda. In Corry (ed.), op cit, pp. 52–54.

Turnbull A. (2004, October 18) Professional skills for government, Launch Event Speech. London.

Tuxworth B. (2001) *LA21: From the Margins to the Mainstream and Out to Sea?* London: Town and Country Planning Association.

Varney D. (2006) *Service Transformation: A Better Service for Citizens and Businesses: A Better Service for the Taxpayer*. London: HMT.

Wainwright H. (2003) *Reclaim the State Experiments in Popular Democracy*. London: Verso.

Wakeford T. (2002, Summer) Citizens juries: a radical alternative for social research. *Social Research Update, no. 37*. Guildford: University of Surrey.

Walker D. (2003) Opinion: is it time to get shot of the civil service? *The Guardian*, 24 October.

Walker D. (2004a, March 3) Introduction to 'Delivering trust'. *The Guardian* (supplement), p. 2.

Walker D. (2004b) The government office for London: does it really fit in? In Corry (ed.), op cit, pp. 29–31.

Walsh K. (1995) Competition and public service delivery. In Stewart and Stoker (eds), op cit, pp. 28–48.

Whiteley P. (2002) *A Health Check for British Governance: What Do We Know about Participation and Its Effects in Britain?* Colchester: University of Essex and ESRC.

Whiteman P. (2004) *The Role of Political Mentors in Local Authorities Recovering from Poor Performance*. London: ODPM.

Widdicombe D. (1986) *Committee of Enquiry into the Conduct of Local Authority Business*. Cmnd 9800.

Wintour P. (2003, January 15) Devolving public services 'must be Labour aim'. *The Guardian*, p. 11.

WLGA (2003) *Improvement in Welsh Local Government*. Cardiff: Welsh Local Government Association.

Wright T. and P. Ngao (2004) *A New Social Contract: From Targets to Rights in Public Services*. London: The Fabian Society.

Young K. and P. Garside (1982) *Metropolitan London: Politics and Urban Change 1837–1981*. London: Edward Arnold.

Zadek S. (2001) *The Civil Corporation: The New Economy of Corporate Citizenship*. London: Earthscan.

Index